for orco— soke,

Conch 2006   Eric

I Remember the Location
Exactly

I Remember the Location
Exactly

Eric Koch

Foreword by Alfred Grosser

mosaic press

National Library of Canda Cataloguing in Publication Data

Koch, Eric, 1919-
    I remember the location exactly / by Eric Koch ; foreword by
    Alfred Grosser.

ISBN 0-88962-861-0

1. Koch, Eric, 1919-. 2. Refugees, Jewish--Germany--Biography.
3. Refugees, Jewish--England--Biography. 4. World War, 1939-1945--
Prisons and prisoners, Canadian. 5. Frankfurt am Main (Germany)--
Biography. 6. Novelist, Canadian (English)--Biography. I. Title.

D811.5.K5942 2006   940.54'8243   C2006-901126-5

Published by Mosaic Press, offices and warehouse at 1252 Speers Road,
Units 1 & 2, Oakville, Ontario L6L 5N5, Canada, and Mosaic Press, 4500
Witmer Industrial Estates, PMB 145, Niagara Falls, NY 14305-1386, USA.

The picture of Frankfurt on the cover is *Eisgang* (1923) by Max Beckmann.
Reproduced with permission of the Städelscher Museums-Verein e.V.,
Frankfurt am Main.

Photo credits:
Rudolf Heilbrunn: by kind permission of Mrs. Trudel Heilbrunn
Otto H. Kahn: John Kobler, *Otto the Magnificent,* Charles Scribner's Sons,
New York 1988
Eric Koch: Dima Chatrov
Ludwig Koch: *Memoirs of a Birdman*, Scientific Book Club, London, 1955

Copyright © 2006, Eric Koch
Printed and bound in Canada.
ISBN 0-88962-861-0

Published by Mosaic Press

In Canada:	In USA:
1252 Speers Road, Units 1 & 2	4500 Witmer Industrial Estates
Oakville, Ontario	PMB 145, Niagara Falls, NY
L6L 5N9	14305-1386
Phone/Fax: 905 825 2130	Phone/Fax 1 800 387 8992

info@mosaic-press.com
www.mosaic-press.com

Other books by Eric Koch

FICTION

The French Kiss
McClelland & Stewart, Toronto, 1969

The Leisure Riots
Tundra Books, Montreal, 1973
Die Freizei Revoluzzer*, Heyne Verlag, Munich

The Last Thing You'd Want to Know
Tundra Books, Montreal, 1976
Die Spanne Leben*, Heyne Verlag, Munich

(*Both German versions were reissued together in 1987 under the title CRUPP.)

Goodnight, Little Spy
Virgo Press, Toronto, and Ram Publishing, London, 1979

Kassandrus
Heyne Verlag, Munich 1988

Liebe und Mord auf Xananta
Verlag Eichborn, Frankfurt, 1992

Icon in Love: A Novel about Goethe
Mosaic Press, Oakville, 1998
Nobelpreis für Goethe, Fischer Taschenbuch, Frankfurt, 1999

The Man Who Knew Charlie Chaplin
Mosaic Press, Oakville, 2000
L'Uomo Chi Splìò Hitler, Barbera Editoré, Siena, 2006

Earrings
Mosaic Press, Oakville, 2002

Arabian Nights 1914: A Novel about Kaiser Wilhelm II
Mosaic Press, Oakville, 2003

NON-FICTION

Deemed Suspect
Methuen, Toronto, 1980

Inside Seven Days
Prentice-Hall, Toronto, 1986

Hilmar and Odette
McClelland & Stewart, Toronto, 1996
Chongqing Publishing House, 1998

The Brothers Hambourg
Robin Brass, Toronto, 1997

Eric Koch

*To my brother, Robert,
in memory of our sister, Margo.*

Contents

Foreword

Alfred Grosser

On October 1, 1937, the president of the French Republic signed a decree granting French citizenship to a number of foreigners. Among those were:

> Rosenthal (Lily Emilie), widow Grosser, born on June 2, 1894, in Frankfurt am Main (Germany), a resident in Saint-Germain-en-Laye, with her two children:
> 1: Margarete, born on April 13, 1922, in Frankfurt am Main
> 2: Alfred Eugen Max, born on February 1, 1925, in id.

Why do I begin this way? First, because of the last given name. The other two were my grandfathers. But Max? That was the name of my mother's first fiancé, Max Koch, who had been killed in the war seven years before I was born. He is mentioned several times in this book and I refer to him, first, because after his death his mother had always regarded my mother as her daughter-in-law. Until 1933, we often visited "Oma Koch" (Grandmother Koch) at her country house in Kronberg. I was afraid of her German shepherd but enjoyed gathering the red currants in her garden.

I refer to him, second, to show how different similar life stories can be. My memoirs, published in 1997, were called *Une vie de Français* (Life of a Frenchman). I was eight when my parents emigrated and was immediately assimilated by my French school. Eric/Otto was twenty at the beginning of the war and was soon after interned in Britain as an enemy alien. In France, the enemy aliens — those who had fled Hitler's Germany — were treated worse. Not only were they interned at the beginning of the war — in the dreadful camp in Gurs, among others — but mainly because, as a result of the shameful Article 19 of the 1940 truce, France had undertaken to deliver to Hitler those who had fled from him.

My becoming French was similar to the Americanization of the refugee children who came to the United States. The best known case is Henry Kissinger, who had left Fürth, in Bavaria, when he was fourteen. I remember a meeting in 1957, at Princeton, with NATO generals, diplomats and other professors. A dispute arose between myself, as a representative of France, and one of the representatives of the U.S., Ernst Haas. He was born in Frankfurt in a street near ours. My father had been his *Kinderarzt* [pediatrician].

Eric/Otto tells how his grandmother could not understand why my parents left Germany in 1933. My father had been removed from his children's clinic; the dean of the University of Frankfurt had "recommended" that he "interrupt" his course of lectures; and the association of veterans who, like he, had been awarded the Iron Cross, had expelled him. He could not know that he would succumb to a heart attack on February 7, 1934, a few weeks after our arrival in France.

A large number of our acquaintances in Frankfurt's Westend thought that only *Ostjuden,* Jews who had recently come from the east, were being threatened, so they stayed. Some who had been able to leave temporarily even returned, to prepare their "legal" emigration. Eric/Otto thinks, in retrospect, that he had been justified in not opposing his mother when she returned to Frankfurt late in 1938. It ended well, but it could easily have ended differently. My father's sister and her husband, a Berlin doctor, spent some time in Switzerland in 1935. Both returned to Berlin and were subsequently deported to Theresienstadt and later murdered in Auschwitz.

Some of the "stories" in this book ended the same way. The reader does not always grasp at first why the story of one person is told in such detail until it becomes clear that a terrible death lends it a special significance, even when the story is full of humour.

But by no means do all the stories end in tragedy. The legend of the descent from Napoleon certainly does not. After all, this is a book of memoirs, occasionally leading to serious, sometimes courageous self-questioning, such as when Eric/Otto asks himself whether he is willing to die a soldier's death or to kill former school friends.

On one subject, the matter of Jewish identity, he might have gone deeper. There is no evidence of any of the Jewish people described having any religious faith, and the Koch family — like mine — seems to have celebrated only the joyful festivals. Being Jewish was a communal matter always strengthened by anti-Semitism. There are many examples in the book of ancient anti-Semitism, but also of the new kind, the Hitler ideology, which owed so much to the *Mitläufertum*, the opportunistic collaboration that was best shown in Eugen Ionesco's play *Rhinoceros*.

As for me, I have always said and written: My father was a pediatrician, a freemason, a voter for the socialist SPD, of *"israelitischer Religion,"* which was the label used at the time. Hitler's finger reduced his identity to a Jewish one. I see no reason why his son should permit Hitler's finger to force the same central identity on him. For me, the essential element was being French, but my German-Jewish identity led me to assume a share of responsibility for the evolution of a democratic Germany. Right at the beginning of the preamble to the French constitution of 1946, it is stated that the victory had been achieved over a "regime that had attempted to enslave and humiliate human beings." Not over peoples or nations. When the first French resistance fighters were deported to Buchenwald and Dachau, they discovered that the concentration camps had been established already in 1933 by Germans for Germans. With the survivors we then began the work of German-French reconciliation.

May I express the hope that another book by Eric Koch will deal with his relationship to the developments in his native country after the war. But for the moment, let us hope that this book will attract many readers. They not only will discover a piece of European and Canadian history, but will also have a most enjoyable time.

Alfred Grosser
Professor Emeritus of Political Science,
L'Institut d'études politiques de Paris
Winner of the Peace Prize of German Publishers, 1975

1

My Conception

I remember the location — exactly.

As you entered the eight-room apartment on the second floor of Rüsterstrasse 20 in Frankfurt, my parents' bedroom was on the far right. To get there you had to pass the carved seventeenth-century armoire in the hall. When you opened its doors lights went on automatically, illuminating my father's collection of antique watches. One of these was made of filigree gold and opened up like a tulip. Opposite the armoire was the dining room dominated by an oil painting of the Frankfurt ghetto by the local painter Anton Burger, proudly placed there in 1911, when my parents moved in, to remind them and their guests — and their future children — how well their ancestors had done since they had emerged from the "Jew Street" about a hundred years earlier. In the dining room there was also a glass cabinet displaying the silver trophies that my father, a passionate horseman, had won in riding tournaments all over Germany before 1914. In 1913 he had established a jumping record of two metres, a record not broken until 1927 by Baron von Buddenbrock.

Next to the dining room there was the *Herrenzimmer*, the smoking room, which, somewhat incongruously, contained my mother's library. Next to it was the music room, also known as *Der Salon*. In it hung, among other paintings, a Montmartre street scene pained by my mother's uncle, Max Kahn. In that room my father, a competent violinist, had often played chamber music with my mother at the piano and her two brothers, Alfred and Emil, playing the violin and cello respectively.

I was conceived in November 1918, shortly after the Kaiser's abdication and flight. The army was disintegrating. Revolution had broken out.

My father, aged thirty-four, had just returned by train directly from northern France. Except for a stint on the Eastern front, he had served in the West throughout the war. He had realized for months that the war was lost. Now, exhausted but unscathed, he was, above all, anxious to see my mother, who was in the waiting room of the railway station.

The train arrived at half past four. The journey had taken sixteen hours. As my father stepped onto the platform a "Red" soldier, much less fierce than my father had expected, pointed with his rifle at his officer's epaulettes and said, almost casually, "Pull them off, or shall I'll have to do it do it for you." This was not St. Petersburg, my father noted to himself.

"Please help yourself," he said with a melancholy smile. ("Always chivalrous but slightly melancholy" were words some of his friends used to describe his behaviour.) Being pleasant to this soldier did not strike him as a betrayal of any principle. He had nothing against people who lived in a world far removed from the world of the court jewellery store Robert Koch in which he was a partner. It had been founded by his father, who had died in 1902. But my father would have been quite willing to admit that, generally speaking, jewellers, especially court jewellers, preferred the upper classes.

The Red soldier snipped off the silver epaulettes with his rifle. Then, with his hand, he removed the Iron Cross First Class from his chest and put it in his pocket.

"You won't need this any more," the soldier said, quite amiably. "What's your name?"

"Otto Koch. What's yours?"

"Wolfgang Rehder."

"Herr Rehder," my father used his officer's voice but deliberately tempered it by speaking not Prussian but the local *frankfurterisch*, "please hand back my order."

The soldier laughed, reached in his pocket and threw it back.

"Now, *viel Vergnügen* — have a good time!" And he added, with a wink, "Your wife's probably waiting."

The Rüsterstrasse was a few blocks away from the station, ten minutes by taxi. To my mother, the fact that Otto had returned alive, after more then four years at the front, was a miracle.

Nothing else mattered, certainly not the Revolution. She was not left a widow, alone with their six-year-old daughter, Margo, and the new baby, Robert. She had endured already enough tragedy. Her brother Alfred had been killed earlier this year, and so had Otto's younger brother, Max.

After Otto washed and put on a civilian suit, father, mother and little Margo, proceeded to my grandmother's apartment in the Unterlindau. Baby Robert had to stay at home with his nanny and the two servants. The Unterlindau was only a few minutes away, just north of the Bockenheimer Landstrasse. Grandmother had sent her car with the chauffeur, Josef Seiter.

Uncle Louis Koch, my grandfather's younger brother and successor at Robert Koch, was there, with his wife, Aunt Alice, who was hard of hearing, and their two grown-up daughters, Martha and Mariechen. Louis was the head of the family and, in effect, my father's boss. Of course, Claire, my father's sister, had come with her husband, the lawyer Ludwig Heilbrunn, and had brought along with them their two teenage sons, Rudolf and Robert, who both worshipped my father. Ludwig was the only politically active member, and the only intellectual in my immediate family. A year later, on the grounds that he believed that, in view of rising anti-Semitism, members of an undesired minority should not occupy positions of prominence in public life, Ludwig resigned from the two political positions he had occupied, one as a liberal-democratic member of the Prussian Legislature, since 1915, and the other as a Frankfurt city councillor, which he had been for twenty years. My mother's mother, Anna Kahn, had also been invited. Llike many other ladies in the West End, she had made her house, just down the street in the Niedenau, available to the city as a *Lazarett*, a combination of hospital and convalescence home.

When my father arrived, my grandmother Koch was sobbing as she embraced her only surviving son, sobbing with joy and with grief for Max. The other ladies kissed him. Louis and Ludwig and the two Heilbrunn boys shook hands.

The table had been set.

"No horse meat for once," said Robert, the younger Heilbrunn boy. He was fourteen and prided himself on his irreverence. Many considered him spoiled. "Good thing Lina has important friends." Lina was the cook and had somehow managed to conjure up a chunk of *Suppenfleisch,* which was served with the local delicacy, *Grüne Sauce,* made of green herbs, eggs and mayonnaise. "But why do we have to have turnips *again?*"

"Please behave, just for once," his mother said, joining in the laughter.

"Did they harass you at the station?" Uncle Louis asked. He had only two daughters, and so my father was the Koch heir. To prepare himself for the future, my father had left high school at sixteen, in the last year of his father's life, to become an apprentice at a jewellery workshop in Hanau. My mother often resented the prominent role Uncle Louis played in her husband's life. On many matters of taste he deferred to his uncle's opinion rather than to hers. Louis was conspicuously extravagant and, in her opinion, took too much delight in his own charm. My mother, by contrast, although beautiful and elegant and in many respects perfectly suited to be a court jeweller's wife, was frugal, bookish, and shied away from any showing-off. Her family, the Kahns, had accumulated their wealth in banking a generation before the Kochs.

"One man tried to make a nuisance of himself," my father said. "But his heart was not in it."

"What happened?" asked Martha, Louis's older daughter. She was married to Willy Dreyfus, a banker who was not at the gathering,

My father described the scene.

"I'm not surprised," Ludwig Heilbrunn said. "It's all rather mild. Unless there are sailors involved. Soldiers' and workers' councils are springing up all over the country, just as they did in Russia last year. But here in most of the councils the Socreds remain in control." The Socreds were the social democrats. "This is not Russia."

"Good," Louis said with feeling. "So they won't cut our throats."

Grandmother Koch did not want to hear any more of such talk.

"Did your friend Rudolf Binding come home with you?" she asked, patting my father's hand. My father had known the patriotic writer and ardent horseman before the war. It was pure coincidence that he had become his superior at the front.

"No, Mother," my father responded. "In September he became dreadfully ill and nearly died. Dysentery and God knows what else. They had to carry him to a field hospital, and then on a stretcher to a train. His footman came along. He has been slowly convalescing in Baden-Baden. I had a few scribbled lines from him two weeks ago. He may be home by now."

"So he could not follow his Kaiser?" the impudent Robert Heilbrunn asked.

"Even if he had been well enough, Robert," my father replied without taking offence, "he would not have done such a thing. He had grave doubts about him, and about the war. For more than a year."

"And so did you, didn't you?" Robert's brother, Rudolf, asked. He was seventeen.

"Yes, I did," my father nodded. This was not the occasion to elaborate. He had never been a flag-waving nationalist, not even during the almost universal enthusiasm at the beginning of the war. Recently, in officers' messes he had to listen to anti-Semitic remarks about "Jewish shirkers and profiteers." He had protested vigorously but to no avail. Such scenes had not tempered his patriotism but caused deep anguish.

"I'll give you two weeks off, my boy," Uncle Louis said amiably, after the dessert of stewed apples. "To catch your breath. And to get to know your wife again."

During those two weeks I was conceived.

2

The Eulogy

Before the war, after a practice jump, my father fell off his horse and dislocated his shoulder. Right through the war his shoulder bothered him. He resolved that, if he survived, he would have it fixed after the war even if it involved surgery. At last, in November 1919, a year after his return, and three months after I was born and named Erich, a surgeon and a bed were ready, notwithstanding hospital overcrowding and the flu epidemic. But something went wrong with the operation. There was a sepsis and, after three days, my father died. Today a simple injection of antibiotics would easily have taken care of it. My mother was twenty-nine.

At the Jewish cemetery at the Rat-Beil-Strasse, standing beside his coffin, his friend and superior officer Rudolf Binding — seventeen years older than my father — delivered the eulogy. He was tall, pale and hollow cheeked and sported a thick, grey mustache.

"I stand before you, my dead comrade," he declared, "asking you to let me celebrate your life in my own way. You would no doubt have preferred a short, muffled volley, or the gentle farewell of the woman you loved. But please let me do it my way.

"I want to tell a story, not because it is about something big but because it is about something small.

"A man went out to war with me. He became my best comrade and my most reliable officer. In Flanders, he rode the first patrol of his division against the enemy. For a whole evening I waited for him to return, and then for a long, long night. Finally I gave up on him. In the early morning I rode out on the road, with poplars on both sides, hoping against hope I would encounter him. And then, in the grey morning mist, there he was, without a helmet, leading a riderless horse by the hand while riding his own. He laughed. Yes, he laughed. He never told me how he acquired that additional horse and I did not ask. I still do not know. Horses do not speak.

"He was a man who was happy when others were happy and who mourned when others mourned. I cannot say anything better of him than that his heart was in the right place. He was a man for whom the good was self-evident and the self-evident good. He found something valuable in every man, however well it may have been hidden.

"You were that man. What has now happened to you is utterly incomprehensible. We like to believe that Fate is governed by secret laws. But not in this case. There cannot have been any secret laws leading to this. Fate itself has suffered a terrible, dreadful accident.

"I cannot part from you without recalling the words of the great pagan poet Plautus: *Quem di diligunt, adolescens moritur.*

"He whom the gods love dies young."

+++

A week after the funeral, Rudolf Binding paid my mother a visit to present her with a handwritten copy of his eulogy, wrapped in tissue paper and tied with a black ribbon. She had never told my father that she had always been indifferent towards his friend. She had read the novels and short stories he had written and found his mannered, perfumed style profoundly unappealing.

Moreover, my mother did not share my father's passion for horses, with which she had associated Binding. It was horses that had brought the two men together. Binding, the son of a wealthy criminal lawyer, had spent the early part of his life at race tracks, running and trading thoroughbred horses. He had not yet begun writing poems and stories. And now that my father's love of horses had led to his death, my mother held Binding somehow responsible. She knew, of course, that this was irrational, but she could not help it.

She received him in the *Herrenzimmer*. He presented his gift. She thanked him and said she had not been able to attend the

7

funeral, but knew that all who heard his story about that mysterious horse had found it deeply moving.

"*Gnädige Frau,*" he began, "if I may, I would like to tell you another story about Otto. I think it would have been inappropriate to tell it at the funeral."

My mother took a deep breath.

"It was late March 1915, in Belgium. Spring had come. Rain and fog had evaporated, the days were growing longer, the sun warmer. As you know, I was a divisional staff officer. Joffre had paralyzed our army and I was not aware of any plan to reverse our fortunes. But that is not what I want to talk about. One day I was told the general commanding one of our infantry brigades needed a new aide-de-camp. The best available candidate by far was Reserve Lance-Sergeant Koch. So I sent him."

"I remember Otto writing to me about this," my mother interjected. "He was very pleased."

"Yes, I think he was. As always, he was admirably efficient and punctilious in carrying out orders. The general was delighted. The general had also noticed very quickly that the horses were in much better shape since Otto had arrived. The general himself was in better shape. He, too, was better looked after. Otto rode with him as he inspected his troops on horseback. Nobody could read maps as well as his new ADC.

"A few weeks later, Otto received the Iron Cross First Class at the recommendation of the general."

"Yes, I remember," my mother smiled.

"Time passed," said Binding. "When the general thought the time had come, he wrote me a letter. He wrote that it was no longer tolerable to allow such an excellent young man to be without having the silver epaulettes of an officer. He had all the qualities that one might require of an officer, he wrote. Therefore, he asked me to recommend Otto for a commission. He would endorse my recommendation."

"Why did he not do it himself?' my mother asked.

"No, no, no. That would have been impossible. As Otto belonged to my squadron I had to make the recommendation. To the Kaiser himself."

"What?" my mother exclaimed. "To the Kaiser? Did that man have nothing better to do than handle every request of this sort?"

"He had to have something to do, you see, *gnädige Frau,* since he had left the conduct of the war to Ludendorff and Hindenburg." Binding sighed. "With highly dubious results, as we have seen. The next day, I put the document personally in the general's hands. He read over all the details — dates, family background, etc. — with the greatest satisfaction. He had not been wrong: the man had led an orderly, in fact, an exemplary life. But suddenly the general froze. Just under the word 'religion' — there could be no mistake about it — it said *Jewish.* Everything that was Prussian in the general, everything that was Christian in him, rebelled. 'Did you know he was a Jew?' the general cried. 'Certainly I knew it,' I replied in an even voice. 'And you still want to go ahead with this?' he asked indignantly. I replied that I could not see why his courage, his usefulness and all the qualities that the general himself had discovered and prized so highly had anything to do with his beliefs. 'Well yes," said the general. 'That is quite true. But you must admit, he has certain qualities, Jewish qualities, which…' I replied that I did not quite see what he meant. The general pondered this for a moment. Then, after a long pause, he ordered me to take back the recommendation. I replied that I regretted very much that I could not do that. He had asked for it and I acted according to my duty and my conscience. The general demurred. But he could not leave the matter alone. He was deeply troubled by it. He discussed it with me every day. I stood my ground. He asked me again and again how I could be so blind as not to see the man's Jewish qualities. In the end he went further. *He said the man had nothing but Jewish qualities.'*

"When he said that, something in me snapped. I decided this had gone far enough. I did not want to embarrass him by asking him once again what exactly were the Jewish qualities he had in mind. 'Yes, sir', I said instead, with some emphasis. 'You are perfectly right, sir. But since he is a Jew why should he have qualities other than Jewish qualities?'

"The general was taken aback. Something had happened to him that he could not fathom. I had suddenly let go of the rope on which he had been pulling. He felt he had fallen down. Without any further delay, he signed the recommendation."

Clearly, Rudolf Binding expected the highest praise for his extraordinary liberalism and quick-wittedness.

My mother looked at him.

"Did Otto know this story?" she asked.

"No, I never told him. It would have been unfair to the general."

My mother shook her head sadly.

There as a moment's silence.

"There are certain things," she said at last, "that I will never understand."

+++

Fourteen years later, in the essay *Antwort eines Deutschen an die Welt* [Reply of a German to the World], published late in 1933, Rudolf Binding welcomed Hitler's assumption of power. The occasion was an article by the French pacifist Romain Rolland asserting that "national-fascist" Germany was the enemy of the true Germany. To make his point he listed many barbarities committed by the Nazis, including barbarities against the Jews. In his reply Binding did not deal with these charges but expressed his scathing contempt for the Weimar republic. He did not specify that he thought the Weimar republic had certain of the Jewish qualities that in 1915 had so worried the general. But one may safely assume that this is the sort of thing he had in mind.

In his defence of Hitler, Binding claimed that every nation had the right to defend its essence. At last a strong Führer had emerged in Germany, he wrote, who would undo the injustices committed at Versailles and would make it possible for Germans, once again, to feel proud.

The murderous events of June 30th, 1934, the Night of the Long Knives, gave him second thoughts. From then on he became increasingly cool towards the Nazis, although he did not object to being in their good graces. It meant a great deal to him that they encouraged young people to read his poems, stories and his war diary, published in 1926, which contained the story about his recommending a Jew to become an officer. He never wavered in his admiration for Thomas Mann and corresponded with him until 1933. But it is significant that he had criticized *The Magic Mountain* when it came out in 1925 as being an un-German novel, too international in concept. But compared to Thomas Mann, Binding knew he was second rate.

In 1935 he submitted the novelist Robert Musil for a grant from a literary foundation and bitterly protested its rejection on the grounds that Musil's wife was Jewish. This did not prevent him, however, from continuing to be an active member of Dr. Goebbels' *Preußische Dichterakademie,* and to allow his work to be used for propaganda purposes, until his death in 1938, as a major German writer.

3

Nix–Nix

"**W**hy are the children so late?"

It was lunch-time on a warm Saturday in the late summer of 1923. Flora Koch, at age sixty-four, dressed in black, was sitting on the veranda of her country house in Kronberg, at the foot of the Taunus Mountains north of Frankfurt, nervously drumming her fingers on the table. She was surrounded by members of the family. Having suffered many blows in her life, she always feared the worst. She never went to bed without kissing the three photographs on her night table, one of her husband, Robert, who had died more than twenty years earlier, and one of her son Max, killed in France early in 1918, and one of her other son, Otto. The wounds had cut so deeply that, in her presence, no one risked speaking of the dead for fear that she might break down.

Her daughter, Claire, looked at her watch.

"It's only twelve," she said. "Let's not start worrying until it's one."

"I'm hungry *now*," Frieda Schwaiger announced. She was a distant, impoverished relative from Munich who was divorced from a mysterious husband no one knew anything about and who rarely allowed an opportunity go by without exercising her wit. She spoke broad Bavarian, which sounded amusing to Frankfurt ears.

Flora Koch smiled. "Go over there, Frieda," she pointed to a jar of cookies, "and help yourself."

"Please bring me one, too," Robert Heilbrunn, now nineteen, ordered. "I'll pay you any price so you can buy yourself a new husband."

Robert enjoyed playing the role of smarty-pants. He had just finished high school and was on his way to Heidelberg to study law, to follow in his father's footsteps. In the morning he had told

Frieda that in the Koch-Heilbrunn family tree only those over a certain income group were listed and she, alas, did not make it.

"Give me three trillion, Robert," she said, laughing.

If this exchange had not taken place in the middle of the German inflation she would merely have said, 'Give me three million.' Prices no longer had any intelligible relation to reality. The hyperinflation that was wrecking the economy was to last until November, when the mark was finally stabilized. By then much of the middle class was ruined. Three paper mills had been working top speed, and one hundred and fifty printing companies had two thousand presses going day and night turning out currency. (Jewellers remained well off because their wealth was based on something more sensible than paper.) To add to these woes, in January the French, alleging delays in the payment of reparations, had occupied the Ruhr, Wiesbaden and parts of the Taunus, including Kronberg, which suddenly became occupied territory. Frankfurt, however, was not.

The reason for everyone's concern was that the French may have kept the three Koch children, Margo, Robert and Otto — whose name was changed from Erich to Otto after his father's death — at the checkpoint in Eschborn, half way between Frankfurt and Kronberg. "Worrying doesn't cure any broken bones," Frieda announced, throwing two cookies across the table in Robert's direction.

This was a reference not to what the French may have done to the three children but to last Saturday's accident when Otto had broken his right arm. He had fallen from the window sill into the salon. Four-year-old Otto had been waiting for Josef Seiter, his grandmother's chauffeur, to arrive as usual with her car. Otto was mature enough to enjoy the expression on people's faces when he told them he had fallen "out of the window."

His mother, Ida, had phoned Kronberg from the hospital. The weekend trip was cancelled.

The three children, guarded by their pretty blond governess, Annelies, spent every summer weekend with their doting grandmother, except during the three-week school holidays when they went with their mother and Annelies to a resort in the mountains or at the seaside. This summer they had gone to the Feldberg in the Black Forest. Because of the constantly rising currency, Frau Koch had to pay the hotel bill twice a day.

"Claire is right, for once," said her husband, Ludwig Heilbrunn. He enjoyed nothing more than teasing his wife. "We shouldn't start worrying until one o'clock. Let's ring the bell and ask Minna to tell Lina we'll have lunch at ten past one.

Minna was the maid, much admired by the two Heilbrunn teenagers for her *gute Figur* — namely, her cleavage — and Lina was the cook. Her bargaining skills on the black market were more impressive than her looks.

"The children are probably late," Claire said, "because Robert had his nose in a book and they couldn't tear him away." She meant the five-year-old Robert Koch, Otto's older brother, not her own son Robert. Both were named after their grandfather.

"I keep thinking of Clem," Flora, the children's grandmother, said. Clem was her older sister. Three weeks earlier the sadistic French had locked her up for two hours in a little hut at the checkpoint in Eschborn, without any ventilation. And without proper facilities. For no reason at all.

"Good thing they didn't execute her," Frieda observed, true to form. "As they did that man Schlageter in Düsseldorf in May."

Leo Schlageter had been condemned to death by a French military tribunal for engaging in sabotage against the French occupation. The German government in Berlin had encouraged the entire population of the occupied territories to engage in non-violent, passive resistance. Schlageter wasn't the only trouble maker. But the French wanted to set an example. Since his execution the extreme right wing celebrated him as a martyr.

"What are you talking about, Frieda?" Flora asked angrily. She had never heard of Schlageter, or of any passive resistance. She only read the local *Generalanzeiger,* which concentrated on disasters in Frankfurt.

"I didn't say *I* would have executed Aunt Clem, Flora," Frieda laughed. "I agree that would be going just a little bit too far."

Ludwig decided the time had come for a change of tone. He addressed himself to Frieda, who he knew was considerably more intelligent than she pretended.

"I make every effort to put myself into the shoes of the French," he declared. "We have devastated their country. It will take two, three generations before they can forgive us. But at the same time they should realize that their vindictiveness makes things worse. That's what the British keep telling them, and the Americans. There are a lot of well-meaning people in France and here in Germany who want to create a new atmosphere by working together."

The veranda was at the back of the house, with an excellent view of the *Altkönig,* the second highest mountain in the Taunus. The front faced the steep Jaminstrasse. The outside gate was not always firmly closed. Anybody could walk in, but then, in order to be let into the house, one had to ring the bell at the front door. What happened next was that two very tall, pitch-black soldiers in French uniform appeared outside the veranda. The gate must have been left unlocked. To infuriate the Germans the French used troops from Senegal as soldiers of occupation.

"*Bonjour,*" they said, smiling.

Robert Heilbrunn was in his element. His school French was excellent.

"Would you gentlemen like to search the house?" he asked eagerly. "Perhaps I can help you — I know where everything is. Are you looking for weapons? For dynamite?"

"We want Minna," one of the soldiers said, grinning.

"Oh, you have made her acquaintance?" Robert asked.

"We have."

Robert asked his grandmother whether she would like to ring the bell to summon Minna.

Flora hesitated.

"Go ahead," Ludwig said to his mother-in-law. "Minna is grown up. She can look after herself."

Flora rang the bell. Minna appeared. She immediately grasped the situation.

"Oh, *bonjour,*" she said. This was practically the only French she knew. She did not seem to be displeased to see the two visitors.

"Come dance with us again this evening, Minna," one of them said to her.

Robert volunteered to translate for her.

"All right," she said, without a moment's hesitation. "But after that — *nix, nix.*"

Those two words were a French version of what the soldiers thought was the German *nichts, nichts,* meaning "nothing doing."

"*D'accord.*" They laughed, no doubt thinking that this was a matter that was open for negotiations.

Minna turned to Flora Koch.

"May I?" she asked.

"You may," Flora responded.

Just as they left Josef Seiter drove the car through the gate and stopped in the driveway. Margo and the two little boys jumped out, ahead of Annelies, who stayed behind to collect the children's belongings. The children ran to the veranda to kiss their grandmother.

"Oh," she gasped with joy. "I was so worried. What happened?"

"The *Barriere* was down in Eschborn," Margo began.

"There was a long, long line-up of cars waiting," Robert continued.

"And then, once it was our turn," Otto broke in, "they arrested Fräulein Annelies!"

"Oh, you don't mean *arrested,*" his grandmother said.

"Oh yes, I do."

He did not mention that the soldiers were the first black men he had ever seen. However, this did not seem to have made any impression on him. He was familiar with black men from the universal children's favourite story *Struwwelpeter.*

At that moment Annelies arrived. She had overheard the last exchange.

"Well, they detained me," she said. "And they would not let me go."

"What did they want from you?" Robert Heilbrunn asked, with an impressive display of innocence.

Annelies blushed.

"They were quite objectionable." She left it at that.

"Did they threaten you in any way?" Ludwig the lawyer asked.

"I don't think that is the word for it." Annelies blushed even more. "Fortunately I remembered my French from school. I kept saying, *"Ne me touchez pas!"*

"But they insisted?" Ludwig asked.

"They only let me go after I had convinced them that I really meant it when I said *nix, nix!*"

+++

Annelies Schwarz, the daughter of a ship's captain in Bremen, stayed with the family until the early 'thirties. Then, for a year or two, she took other jobs. Around 1937 she joined her Jewish lover in Paris. After the outbreak of war, the French interned her, but, for some reason, not him, as an enemy alien in Gurs in southwest France. After the French collapse, when the Germans came they deported him. He was never heard from again. After her release she went underground and in 1946 went to New York to live with her sister. Once in the States she again became close to our family. After her sister died, Annelies lived alone until her death in the 'eighties.

4

The Vampire

The time was April 1926 and the scene the Frankfurter Hof, Frankfurt's ritziest hotel.

After his bath, Otto H. Kahn, an American cousin of my mother's father, was having his breakfast in his suite, reading the newspaper. His valet, Freddy, was laying out his clothes for the day when a uniformed boy knocked at the door and presented an unstamped letter on a silver tray. Freddy passed it on. Otto H (as he was universally known) opened it and read it. It was signed by Albrecht Holberg, a name that sounded vaguely familiar. It was written in a beautiful hand.

> Dear Mr. Kahn,
> I don't expect you to remember me but long, long ago we were classmates at elementary school in Mannheim. After that we were in the same regiment when we did our military service in Mainz in 1887. I have followed your career as a financier and philanthropist with admiration, and even a degree of envy. I know that you are a celebrity who knows everybody of importance, including Charlie Chaplin, and that your country house has one hundred and twenty-seven rooms and that you employ as many servants.
> As a modest pharmacist in Ginnheim I have no complaints about my own condition in life. But I must confess that I occasionally boast to my customers that we used to know each other.
> I am writing to you to draw your attention to the possibility of some unpleasantness during your remaining days in Germany. Frankly, I am surprised you did not

run into any trouble, as far as I know, while you were in Berlin. Many of us have long memories. There are many Germans who were deeply offended by the reports of your anti-German speeches in the years preceding America's intervention in the war and your efforts to move American public opinion in that direction. Even more objectionable was the letter you wrote to your brother-in-law in Berlin in 1915, which the French authorities intercepted, copied and dropped over German trenches in order to demonstrate to their enemies that a former German citizen had recognized the truth about the "fatherland." No wonder the Kaiser asked for your assassination.

I myself saw that letter; I don't remember where. Your brother-in-law had complained about the lies in the British press about German atrocities in Belgium, and about the ignorance in England and France about Germany generally, its superior levels of education, efficiency and culture, and its high ethical standards. In your reply you conceded the point about German efficiency. But you also charged that, by reason of this very efficiency, Germany was well on the way to achieving economic supremacy in Europe. Why then resort to arms, you asked, to achieve something that could have been achieved peacefully?

To many of us, including myself, this question ignored the basic truth that the allies were determined to prevent such supremacy at all costs by force.

Though I strongly disagreed with your views then, and presumably now, I would never do more than declare my willingness to debate these matters with you. Others would prefer more radical means. There is a rising tide of fanaticism in Germany today.

If I were you I would ask for police protection during your remaining time in Germany.

With very good wishes,
Albrecht Holberg

Only fools ignore letters like this, Otto H said to himself. He phoned the desk and asked whether the general manager had a few minutes to spare. While waiting for him he scribbled a cordial note of thanks to Albrecht Holberg and gave it to Freddy to dispatch.

The general manager came immediately and read the letter. Otto H was reminded of the last Don Basilio he had seen at the Met.

"There is no need for any additional steps," the general manager assured him. "Whenever we have advance notice of a visit from a prominent political person from abroad we notify the authorities. You are already under police protection. Nothing will happen to you."

German efficiency, even in the Weimar republic, Otto H thought.

"You mean nothing will happen to me unless it's pleasant?" he asked.

"Of course." The general manager smiled.

"Well, that is good to know."

"Oh, by the way," the general manager said, "the concierge has received several requests from reporters asking for an interview. What are your instructions?"

"Sorry, no interviews this time," Otto H replied. He had said all he needed to say in Berlin. He was in Frankfurt on business and to meet with old relatives. He also intended to go to the Städel, the art gallery, and to see *Tristan and Isolde* tomorrow, the first opera to which his parents had taken him at the age of eleven. There was hardly any need to add that he had a special relation to this opera because, during the 1908–09 season of the Metropolitan Opera in New York, a major row erupted when Toscanini conducted it while Gustav Mahler, who had also been engaged by the Met, had been led to consider it his territory. As chairman of the board and the man who regularly covered its deficits, Otto H took full responsibility for the decision. During the next season, the Met lost Mahler, who henceforth conducted only the New York Philharmonic orchestra until he returned to Vienna with very mixed feelings about America.

The general manager left and Otto H began dressing. This took him the better part of an hour. He was known for his sartorial splendor, for his vests trimmed with white piping and his pearl-grey spats. Freddy had already found him a red rose for his buttonhole. At fifty-nine Otto H was still a handsome man, with a smooth oval face, white hair, bright light-brown eyes and a white mustache waxed to fine points. There was a strong family resemblance between him and most of the descendants of the brothers Bernhard and Hermann Kahn, both Mannheim bankers. The first, Bernhard, was the father of Otto H and seven others, and the second, Hermann, opened a branch in Frankfurt and became the father of twins and Otto Koch's grandfather. A sharp eye could detect a certain family resemblance between Otto H and Ida Koch, Otto's mother. Most of the Kahns had an interest in the arts.

He told the concierge he was leaving for the Städel in case anybody called, left the Frankfurter Hof and strolled one block westward along the Kaiserstrasse. Whenever he was seen on Fifth Avenue, he was immediately recognized and often accosted, but here, and in Berlin, he was not a public figure, and it was a pleasure for him just to wander about *incognito,* as it were, and admire the elegant ladies, and perhaps even more the not so elegant ladies, and to look at the shop windows. Presumably he was followed by a policeman, but he never bothered to turn around and look. At the corner of the Neue Mainzer Strasse was the building of the court jeweller Robert Koch, a building, he had read somewhere, that had been designed by Paul Wallot, the architect of the Reichstag. He remembered vaguely that a granddaughter of his late uncle Hermann had married into that family, but that was not enough reason to go in. He found that, as far as he could tell, the broaches, bracelets and pearl necklaces displayed in the window were fully up to the standards of Tiffany's and Cartier.

He knew the city well. He went south on the Neue Mainzer Strasse, crossed the bridge across the river Main, then turned right and walked along the Schaumainkai to the Städel, one of his favourite art galleries. He went in, wondering for a moment whether the policeman would follow him or wait outside, and gave his name to the man at the reception desk and asked whether Dr. Georg Swarzenski, the director, was in. He had met the internationally renowned art historian and medievalist on a number of occasions. Collectors in Europe and the U.S. frequently consulted him before acquiring new works, and he was well acquainted with Otto H's treasures, such as Frans Hals's *Family Group,* for which he paid a record-breaking $500,000 at Christie's in London in 1910, outbidding Pierpont Morgan, and Rembrandt's *Portrait of a Young Student,* which he had bought from a dealer in St. Petersburg for a mere $150,000 in the same year.

Yes, Dr. Swarzenski was in and delighted to see him. They exchanged gossip from the art world. Suddenly an idea occurred to Otto H. He was curious to know, he said, what he thought of his cousin, the artist Max Kahn whom he was going to see that evening, the first time since before 1914.

"The painter of *The Vampire?*" Dr. Swarzenski smiled.

"Oh? I have not heard of it. What an astounding subject for him."

"It certainly is. Where are you going to meet him?"

"At his late twin brother Bernhard's house in the Niedenau. We will both be the guests of Bernhard's widow, Anna Kahn."

"In that case the first thing you'll see is *The Vampire.* In the foyer, right at the entrance. A most extraordinary picture. The almost transparent whitish-green flesh of the naked lady under attack is quite remarkable."

"If Max is such a good painter why aren't there any of his works in your gallery?"

"Because, alas, your cousin suffers from arrested development. He never caught up even with the Impressionists, let alone with any more recent style. He's a charming, gifted anachronism. I've met him several times. And his beautiful wife, Thérèse, too, who was his model and mistress in Paris, in the naughty 'nineties. But he never got beyond Jean-François Millet and his peasants. The only interesting, truly original and important picture of his I've seen is *The Vampire.* The rest, as I say, is very ordinary."

Otto H stroked his white mustache as he pondered an idea. "Do you think I should buy it from Anna?"

Dr. Swarzenski laughed.

"You can try."

At that moment the secretary, a dignified tall lady with glasses, interrupted.

"A ... gentleman is here who is anxious to see Mr. Kahn. He says he had some trouble dissuading a policeman from arresting him on his way up."

Dr. Swarzenski frowned. By her manner, his secretary had made it clear that the gentleman was not a gentleman.

"The police?"

Otto H explained.

"I see." Dr. Swarzenski paused to think. "Shall I let him in?"

"Why not? If you have the time. Perhaps you could ask your secretary to offer the policeman a chair."

A man appeared who strongly reminded Otto H of Charlie Chaplin's tramp. Did he also go to school with me? Otto H wondered.

"I am Gerhard Wallach," he said in a broad Baden voice. "I was born in Stebbach."

"Oh really?" Otto H was amused. He explained to Dr. Swarzenski that Stebbach was a small village not far from Heilbronn. "So was my father."

"That's why I've come to see you, Mr. Kahn. Don't worry. I am not a *Schnorrer.* I will not ask you for money. Even though I've lost everything in the inflation and am now working in a garage."

"I see."

"I'm also Jewish," the tramp added.

Otto H wished he hadn't said that. Of course, the use of the word *Schnorrer* had already made that apparent. He had no use for people who advertised their Jewishness. He was very much aware that in his case it was an obstacle to his reaching the top of New York society, that many doors remained closed. As a matter of fact, he was considering becoming a Catholic, for this and for aesthetic reasons. But he could not bring himself to take the final step.

"There weren't many Jews in Stebbach in our fathers' day," he observed.

"There were some," the tramp said. "The Wallachs, for example." But he did not wish to follow this up. "They wouldn't let me in the hotel, so I came here. I want to ask you a simple question.

What would your rich gentile friends in America say if they knew that your father had been condemned to death for taking part in a revolution?"

Otto H smiled. He was, above all, an American patriot, a Republican, an advisor to presidents. "My friend, they would congratulate me. They would say they owed their freedom to their ancestors who had also fought in a revolution."

"That's not what I hear, Mr. Kahn. I hear they don't like Jewish revolutionaries. And nor do you."

Otto H could not deny that.

"The point is," the tramp continued, "that it was unspeakable misery that had led to the revolution in Baden. There had been crop failure after crop failure. There was starvation and despair. Thousands decided to emigrate to America. And whose fault was all this? The Jews, they said. We had a terrible time. So naturally, young Jews were among the most ardent revolutionaries."

"Yes, I know," Otto H said in a tired voice.

He knew perfectly well that both his father, Bernhard, and his uncle Hermann, aged twenty-one and eighteen respectively, had been activists in the revolution of 1848. In his childhood he heard many horror stories about the Prussians who were called in to put down the revolution. They did so with great brutality. That was one reason why ever since he had detested the Prussians. The two brothers managed to escape across the Swiss border. They were tried and convicted *in absentia*.

"Times change," he said, lamely.

Otto H turned to Dr. Swarzenski. "It was a short step from bedfeathers to banking," he explained. "With a short pause for revolution. My father and his siblings worked with their parents in their bedfeather processing plant in Stebbach. They'd started it in their back yard. They did well. They were enterprising. They soon discovered Hungarian geese had the best feathers, so they imported them. In earlier times only kings and queens could sleep on pillows filled with feathers. Thanks to us Kahns everybody could. A few years after the revolution they moved to Mannheim and added banking to bedfeathers. And in Mannheim they soon started their life in the arts."

"So I have heard. I understand Brahms always stayed with them when he was in Mannheim and they endowed a public library," Dr. Swarzenski said.

"That's absolutely right," Otto H smiled. "In the next generation my uncle Hermann and his wife, Henriette, had twins, my cousins Bernhard and Max. They were rich enough to allow one of them, Max, to become a painter, a normally highly unremunerative profession. His banking twin, Bernhard, now unfortunately deceased, agreed to support him, without hesitation. I understand this impressively civilized arrangement between the twins made it possible for Max to paint the picture I'm going to buy tonight."

+++

That evening, *The Vampire* was the first thing Otto H saw after the maid had let him into Anna Kahn's house. It was certainly stunning. But did he really like it? He had a reputation for going against the trend, for taking risks. He had backed many a theatre show that had flopped on Broadway. But was this picture really as significant as Dr. Swarzenski said? Should he go through with his idea and make a bid for it?

He decided he would.

He had forgotten what a lovely, dignified, witty man his cousin Max was, and how impressive-looking he was, with his white goatee and his unusual posture, the shoulders pulled back and the stomach forward. He looked very French, a little old fashioned, like a figure out of an Anatole France novel. At the same time he was reminded of his father. (Otto H and Max were exactly the same age.) As he listened to him at the dinner table, it seemed at times as though he heard his father talking.

But he had some difficulty making contact with Thérèse, whom he had not met before. He insisted on speaking to her in French but she was unresponsive. He only found out later that Max had told her all kinds of salacious stories about his mistresses. Some of them were perhaps even true. He had no idea who might have told them to Max. Considering her own past, Thérèse was singularly puritanical.

Otto H had met Anna before the war but hardly remembered her. They had little in common. She had been born in Bühl, a small town in the Black Forest near Baden-Baden, and had remained a small-town girl all her life. She was the daughter of a once prosperous manufacturer who lost his business after the Franco-Prussian war, when he could no longer keep up with his competitors in Alsace, which had suddenly become German.

"Don't you think, my dear Anna," Otto H said, with a wink at Max, "that we should all envy Max for being able to devote his entire life to the pursuit of beauty?"

"Absolutely," she said, a little uncertain why Otto H was saying this. "I've never begrudged it to him."

"I personally think," Max declared solemnly and emphatically, "that making money is vulgar."

"I totally agree," Otto H shot back. "It just happens to be the only thing I do well. I wish I had your talent, Max. I used to play the cello, but I was no good."

"But I understand you manage to pursue beauty in your own fashion," Max observed.

"Yes, that is true. I have bought a few nice things in my time."

"That is not what I mean at all," Max said. "I hear that in your mansion on Fifth Avenue in New York there are a number of private rooms reserved for the purposes of your entertaining beautiful young singers, dancers and actresses who want to further their careers. I mean, what's the use of all that money you've made unless you can invest it in activities that give you pleasure?"

"Please, Max," Anna said, horrified.

"My dear Max," Otto H replied. "I encourage young talent in any way I can. Now let me ask you this. Who was the model you used for the splendid picture I saw in the foyer?"

"You mean *The Vampire?* Thérèse, of course. Who else?"

"Anna," he turned to his hostess. "I would like to buy *The Vampire* from you."

"You would?" Anna could not believe her ears. "That's up to Max." For years her family had been poking fun at the picture. They had called it *Kitsch.* "I would certainly not accept a single pfennig for it."

"Do you mean," Thérèse asked Otto H, "you want to hang the picture in your house in New York?"

"Yes, of course, " Otto H replied amiably. "Why not? It would be in very good company."

"Max," she said to her husband, almost in tears. "You must not allow that!"

"And why not, *ma chérie?*"

"Now that you have told them it's me I simply could not abide it if your cousin looked at me every day!"

"Thérèse always has the last word," Max declared, patting his wife's hand. "That settles it. *The Vampire* stays here."

+++

Otto H. Kahn died in New York in 1934.

Max Kahn died in Carpentras, France, in 1939. Thérèse survived the war.

My grandmother Anna Kahn was deported from Frankfurt to Theresienstadt in September 1942, and died there three months later.

5

Napoleon and I

Whenever I need attention I tell this story:
Do you remember the Battle of Jena on October 14, 1806, when Napoleon beat the Prussians? He had already beaten the Austrians a few times and made himself Emperor. The Russians and English were to come next. You don't remember? Well, take it from me — he did beat the Prussians at Jena. And to celebrate his victory Napoleon did what he always did after a victory: he had his men seek out the most beautiful girl in the neighbourhood to help him celebrate. That was at a time when he had one or two victories each week.

So naturally they picked my great great grandmother Red Esther, the wife of Shmuel, also known as Long Esther because she had red hair and was so tall. Nobody knows what the family did for a living. They spoke a form of Yiddish known as *Jargon*, written with Hebrew letters. They were poor but not very poor because their house in Stadtlengsfeld, not far from Jena, had an oven. Hence, when some members of the family had a chance to choose German names to take the place of their Hebrew names, they picked *Backhaus*, baking house. (The great pianist Wilhelm Backhaus [1884–1969], who apparently did not mind playing for the Nazis, was a descendant. Please don't ask me whether he knew anything about the "non-Aryan" blood flowing in his veins.) Shmuel, however, agreed with his far-sighted wife, who suggested they pick the neutral name *Koch* [cook] for the rest of the family rather than an identifiable Jewish name, so their children would have an easier time. Esther was obviously a bright lady with an eye to the future who would not allow any opportunity go by unseized.

So on this day Napoleon's men knocked at the Koch door. Shmuel opened it. They asked whether they could see Madame,

28

please. By all means, said Shmuel. Napoleon's men then issued an invitation to Madame — to Madame only — to meet His Majesty at a party at some requisitioned mansion, not far away. They would come to pick her up.

"Who else will be there?" Shmuel needed to gain time while wondering whether there was any way to stop his wife.

"Oh, all the usual people," Napoleon's men said.

Shmuel decided there was no way to stop her, so he might as well give in gracefully.

"In that case," he said to Esther, "why not go? You might meet somebody you know."

"What am I going to wear?" Esther wondered.

"I don't think it matters," Shmuel said, correctly.

After the horse-drawn wagon deposited Esther at the mansion, she was shown into a waiting room. Everything followed a carefully worked-out procedure. Not a moment was wasted. The situation was entirely clear. A maid accompanied her to a bedroom.

"May I help you take off your dress?" she asked. "And everything else?"

"No, thanks," Esther said. "I think I can manage by myself."

"In that case, once you've taken everything off, you must lie down on this bed and wait for His Majesty. He will come when he is ready."

Esther did not bring along needlework to keep herself busy, so all she could do while waiting was stare at the rococo ceiling.

After about half an hour Napoleon arrived, followed by an aide-de-camp, who carried a pad and pencil. She was surprised how small the Emperor was. There was no language problem because all he said was *"Bonjour, madame,"* and she understood that. Then he grunted. That presumably meant he was pleased with what he saw. He took off the top of his uniform and undid his breeches while dictating the orders for the next day's military activities. He continued his dictation while joining her on the bed. He only stopped for a minute while the aide-de-camp discreetly looked out of the window. When he was finished he said, *"Merci, madame."*

She got dressed and was given a ride home.

"How was it?" asked Shmuel.

"Oh, just the usual thing," she replied.

Nine months later my great grandfather was born. How do I know he was my great grandfather? Because at the age of sixteen he went to Leipzig to study medicine. Now, where would a poor Jewish boy get the funds to go to Leipzig to study medicine except from the Bonaparte family in Paris?

+++

Many Jewish families fabricated similar legends in the areas conquered by Napoleon. He had brought the French revolution to the rest of Europe and opened the ghettos. Who would not wish to be descended from the great liberator?

My great grandfather, Dr. Hermann Koch, spent his entire life as a country doctor in Geisa, near Stadtlengsfeld. He never claimed to be Napoleon's son. The legend was created by members of the next generation and taken seriously enough for one uncle to gather a major collection of Napoleon's letters and for one aunt to detect a strong resemblance between herself and Napoleon's sister Pauline.

It was a sad day for the Kochs when somebody inspected Dr. Koch's grave in the Jewish cemetery in Stadtlengsfeld and discovered he was born on December 4, 1808. nearly twenty-six months after the Battle of Jena.

6

Queen Victoria and I

Soon after she became queen in 1837 Victoria decided to marry her cousin Albert. He was assumed to be the second son of Grand Duke Ernest of Saxe Coburg (not far from Jena).

In 1934 Laurence Housman published the play *Victoria Regina,* which became a great success on Broadway when Helen Hayes played the queen. In England the Lord Chamberlain did not permit a performance because it presented members of the royal family who were still alive. But another reason may have been that it contained a scene that stated that Lord Melbourne, the prime minister, only allowed Victoria to marry Albert because he was *not* the son of Grand Duke Ernest. There had been reports that the Grand Duke was suffering from an unnamed and undesirable disease.

Mr. Tudor, British Minister at the Court of Saxe-Coburg Gotha
If your Lordship wishes to prevent the marriage with Prince Albert, it can be done quite easily.

Lord Melbourne
I've been trying all I know how.. And it's God damn difficult. She shut me down — as if I were nobody. I've tried more than once.

Tudor
It need not be difficult, my Lord. You have merely to state certain facts, and — the match will be off.

Melbourne
Well, now you do interest me, exceedingly! Already morganatically married to some German wench, eh?

Tudor
Oh, no, no. Nothing of that sort. The Prince has a blameless character. The same cannot be said about his late mother, the Duchess.

Melbourne
No, so I ... Her parents separated over something, I believe.

Tudor
They separated when the Prince was five years old. She went to live in Paris; he never saw her again. The cause of the separation was of more than five years' standing, my Lord. (This is said with meaning).

Melbourne (rising, with sharp interest)
Heh? ... You don't say so!

Tudor
After five years the parties forgot to be prudent: the thing got about.

Melbourne (sitting down)
Who was — the other party?

Tudor
One of the Court Chamberlains: a very charming and accomplished person, but a commoner, and of Jewish extraction.

Melbourne (pondering deeply)
Dear me! Dear me! ... Healthy?

Tudor
Oh, quite ... You have only to tell Her Majesty that her cousin, Prince Albert, is not quite so much her cousin as she imagines, and I apprehend that you will have no further difficulty.

+++

In 1926 my sister, Margo, was fourteen years old. Her best friend and schoolmate was Yella (Gabriele) von Meyer, who lived opposite us. Yella happened to be related to us through her elderly and aloof father, Baron von Meyer, the brother of Gertrud Flersheim whose husband, Ernst, was a first cousin of my grandmother Koch. In our family that was a close relationship. Tante Gertrud, who was lovable but somewhat scatterbrained, visited us often — she usually came unannounced. In fact, it was a running joke. Whenever the bell rang we said "Aha! Tante Gertrud!"

Margo and Yella walked along the Westendstrasse to the Viktoriaschule together.

Margo
Oh, by the way, why is your father a baron?

Yella
He just is. That's all there is to it.

Margo
Was his father a baron, too?

Yella
Probably.

Margo
And are all Barons vons?

Yella
Yes. That goes together.

Margo
Are there some vons who are not barons?

Yella
Why are you asking me all these silly questions?

Margo
Because I read somewhere that all you had to do to become a baron was to pay the Kaiser a few thousand marks.

Yella
That is not true. Anyhow, the Kaiser had nothing to do with it. My father was born in Coburg. And it was his grandfather who was made a von. Not by any Kaiser. But by the Grand Duke of Saxe-Coburg.

Margo (laughing)
Why? Did he pay him a few thousand marks?

Yella
I have no idea.

+++

Laurence Housman assumed that Tudor, whoever he was, was right. So did Lord Melbourne who preferred a Jew to a Grand Duke with an undesirable disease. The particular Jew under discussion was Baron von Meyer, the grandfather of Yella's father, who, like dozens of other Court Jews at German courts headed by impoverished princes, provided the credit that made it possible for them to operate, and, in the case of Saxe-Coburg-Gotha, to provide ambitious and intelligent princes to the thrones of Europe.

This tiny, sleepy, insignificant principality was in particular need of such services. Its only industry was the court. While occupied by Napoleon it was so poor that the Grand Duchess had to burn her bedroom furniture to keep warm. The principality entered the world stage only when Charlotte, daughter of George IV, Victoria's aunt and successor to the English throne, fell in love with Albert's gifted and handsome uncle Leopold, the future King of Belgium. She met him in London and married him in 1816 against the wishes of her father. Her death in childbirth a year later ended Leopold's chance to become Prince Consort.

Tudor's information was based on mere gossip. There had been objections to Victoria marrying a first cousin. News that Albert was not the Grand Duke's son took care of that, whoever the father was. As it turned out, Tudor and Melbourne were wrong: Albert *was* the Grand Duke's biological son and did not inherit, or ever catch, any undesirable disease.

Victoria and Albert had innumerable descendants. Today they occupy all remaining throne in Europe except the few taken by others.

I would have relished being related to them.

+++

At the gate of Myliusstrasse 32 in Frankfurt there is this plaque:

In this house Clara Schumann died on May 20, 1896

The house belonged to Ernst and Gertrud Flersheim, who perished in Belsen in 1945.

7

Miami

Rudolf Heilbrunn's heart was in books, especially in his collection of first editions by the philosopher Spinoza, not in the law, in which he had recently received his doctorate in Heidelberg, and certainly not in jewellery. However, in the mid 'twenties, family considerations forced him to become a partner in Robert Koch. The head of the firm was Uncle Louis, a charming, charismatic autocrat, a man in his late fifties who had the useful and ingratiating habit of treating whomever he was dealing with as the most important person in the world. When dealing with royalty, ex-royalty or the very rich he was never obsequious and, as a democrat, philanthropist and prominent member of the Jewish community, he considered himself to be the moral equal of anybody. He drew a solid line between his customers and his family — none of his customers was ever invited to his home to dinner at his and Aunt Alice's lovely house in the Kettenhofweg, with its fine collection of paintings and china.

The occasion for this story is the visit of a lady who said she was Princess Lubka Enesco, Lady-in-Waiting to Her Majesty, Queen Marie of Rumania, and the way Rudolf and Uncle Louis responded.

Rudolf was genetically conditioned to know a great deal about the European aristocracy, just as Court Jews had been in previous centuries. He had never heard of this lady or her family. All he knew was that Queen Marie had played a major role during the peace negotiations in Paris in 1919, was a granddaughter of Queen Victoria and was estranged from King Ferdinand.

This is what happened.

An overdressed Rumanian dowager walked into the Robert Koch store and declared she wished to inspect an assortment of tiaras and black pearl necklaces.

Rudolf Heilbrunn asked the dowager to accompany him to the Kaiser Room in the back, reserved for celebrity customers and those who, like this dowager, behaved like one. The room was decorated with charters and patents from Edward VII of England, King Umberto of Italy and at least a dozen German sovereigns. The Kaiser had never been in the Kaiser Room. He rarely came to Frankfurt because the city was run by social democrats.

Rudolf showed the dowager a selection. She liked one tiara in particular. "How much is it?" she asked.

"A hundred thousand," Rudolf replied.

"I would like to show it to my husband before I make a decision," she said. "He is not well. Could you please send it along to the Frankfurter Hof? Let's say, at three this afternoon, after his nap. We are in Suite 336. And leave it with us for a couple of days."

She gave him her card — not a common practice in the nobility, very unorthodox, in fact — and swept out of the store.

Obviously it was essential that Rudolf report this matter to Uncle Louis right away, even before he did the necessary research about her. But first he would send for his distant relative Frieda Schwaiger, the source of a great deal of gossip about the nobility.

There was one thing he was certainly *not* going to do. He was not going to send the tiara to the Frankfurter Hof, at three o'clock this afternoon, after Prince Enesco's nap.

After all, Rudolf knew the Miami story.

Some time around 1908 or 1909, a man claiming to be an American millionaire, obviously considerably more confidence-inspiring than this Rumanian dowager, had a diamond necklace sent to the Frankfurter Hof under similar circumstances. He told one of the sales people there was no need to be concerned because it would be placed in the hotel's safe when he had to go out. He assured the salesman that he would not leave it in his room under any circumstances.

It proved to be a monumental mistake to believe anything the imposter said. He and the diamond necklace vanished. There was evidence that he had given it to the hotel staff to be placed in the safe on his way out, which raised the question of negligence by them. An insurance company became involved, and so did the police. It was soon discovered that the man had gone to Hamburg and quickly embarked by steamer for New York. A young Koch partner — my father, Otto Koch, in fact — was asked to follow him on another steamer, and in due course, through ingenious detective work, my clever father found the villain *and the necklace* in Miami. At Koch in Frankfurt nobody had ever heard of Miami. What happened to the villain was not known and is irrelevant. What is known is that Otto Koch returned to Frankfurt in triumph. Since then, whenever anybody suspicious appeared in the Koch store, the code word was Miami.

Back to the case of Princess Lubka. Rudolf knocked at Uncle Louis's door, was called in and found that his uncle was deep in conversation with Klaus Trautmann, a dealer in old autographs, manuscripts and documents, a scholarly man whom Rudolf knew and liked. Rudolf made his report, adding the code word Miami.

"Good boy," Uncle Louis said and slapped him on the back. "We'll have to confer later on how to handle the lady. I thought you were going to tell me the King of Siam had dropped in."

"What's this about the King of Siam?" Trautmann asked.

Rudolf wanted Uncle Louis to concentrate on Princess Lubka but he could not stop him. He had heard the story about the King of Siam a hundred times.

"Let me tell you," Uncle Louis said to Trautmann. "About twenty years ago, King Chulalongkorn appeared at our store in Baden-Baden, fully equipped with his Malacca cane, and accompanied by an aide. As you no doubt know, he was the ninth son of King Mongku."

"Oh yes, of course," Herr Trautmann said.

"His Majesty pointed with his cane at everything he saw in the window and in the glass cases in the store. That simple gesture meant he wanted it. After he left, we were sold out. The aide paid cash. Not even one tiny little gold bracelet was left. We usually keep a few of those in stock, to give as presents to little princesses. Either real princesses, or ex-princesses, or dollar princesses. But not fake princesses."

"A disaster!" Herr Trautmann chuckled. "You had to fill the glass cases, shelves and windows all over again, from the very beginning."

"Exactly. Terrible. Terrible. Now let me show you," he turned to Rudolf, "what Herr Trautmann is offering me."

If Princess Lubka had not been Rudolf's prime preoccupation at the moment he would have been fascinated. But it was clear he could not get Uncle Louis's attention.

"Prince Adalbert of Mecklenburg-Lausitz," Trautmann said, "had bad luck in the inflation. He was forced to sell many of his treasures. Have a look."

Uncle Louis had a collection of musical autographs that was already one of the greatest in Europe. It contained Bach's cantata *Gott, wie dein Name,* Mozart's opera *The Impresario*, Schubert's *Die Winterreise* and *The Trout* and his last three piano sonatas, not to mention Beethoven's Piano Sonata in A Major Opus 101 and the Diabelli Variations, Opus 120. When the pianist Arthur Schnabel came to town he always visited Uncle Louis, just to hold some of these manuscripts in his hands.

Klaus Trautmann picked up a letter written by Mozart to his sister, after their father died, dated August 1, 1787, dealing with the inheritance. Then there was another Mozart letter, written a year later to his friend Michael Puchberg, asking for a loan, adding in a postscript — "when will we meet again to make a little *musique?* I have just written a new trio." This was a reference to the Trio in E-flat major, K. 542, Trautmann said. Then he showed them an undated letter by Beethoven to the pianist Marie Bigot, inviting her and her little daughter to a pleasure ride because the weather was so *himmlisch*, so divine, and another letter by Beethoven, written in February 1814, to the singer Anna Milder-Hauptmann for whom he had written the role of Leonore in *Fidelio*. She had asked him to compose a concert aria for her to be sung in the *Redoutensaal*. For this, unfortunately, Beethoven wrote, he did not have the time.

Uncle Louis turned to Rudolf.

"The Prince wants ten thousand for the whole lot," he said in a voice suggesting that he thought this was low. "What do you think?"

"Pay it," Rudolf said.

"I always do what my nephew says," Uncle Louis said to Trautmann.

At this moment Frieda Schwaiger was shown in. Uncle Louis liked her. He knew he would not be interrupted unless there was an important reason.

"Frieda! To what happy event do we owe this pleasure?" He introduced her to Trautmann as "my favourite cousin."

"I hope you came in through the back entrance." He couldn't abide it if members of the family came in the same way as the customers.

"You owe this to the dropping from heaven of Princess Lubka Enesco, Lady-in-Waiting to Her Majesty Queen Marie of Rumania." This sounded bizarre in Frieda's native Bavarian. "Rudolf, you're a genius to have asked me. The lady has a good, solid Frankfurt background. Prince Carol Enesco is her third husband. Her maiden name was Levinsohn. She lived opposite the Kochs in the Uhlandstrasse. Her name is Sarah."

"I don't believe it!" Uncle Louis shouted. "Sarah Levinsohn!"

Rudolf had rarely seen his uncle so excited.

"It was because of her," he nearly cried with joy, "that I was thrown out of the *Philanthropin* [The Jewish high school]. I must have been about fourteen. She was irresistible. On several occasions I took her to the birds' cage in the Zoo in the evenings, after it was closed. Climbed over the fence. I was amazed how well she managed that, in her long skirt. We had a very good time in the birds' cage. But then her mother found out and went to the director and complained. She may first have gone to my mother, too. No doubt she wouldn't believe her little Louis was capable of such a thing." He paused, scratching the back of his head. "Why didn't Sarah come and see me directly, instead of going in the store?"

"Obviously she has forgotten you *and* the birds' cage," Frieda replied.

"Impossible!" cried Uncle Louis.

"Uncle Louis," Rudolf asked, "did you, or did you not open the vulture cage, while you were about it, and let all the vultures fly all over Frankfurt?"

"I did not! I have always denied it," he insisted. "Malicious gossip, spread by my many enemies." He turned to Herr Trautmann.

"I was eight years old when my brave and enterprising mother brought her daughter and her four sons to Frankfurt, after our father's death in 1870. We had no money. Our father was a poor country doctor in Geisa who often forgot to charge his patients. Everybody worshipped him. But you can't live on that. When we came to Frankfurt, we had a small apartment on the Hanauer Landstrasse. Then we moved to the Uhlandstrasse. My older brothers got jobs as soon as they had finished the *Einjährige*, when they were fifteen."

There was an interruption. Princess Lubka Enesco had returned to the store, asking to see Dr. Heilbrunn.

"Well?" Frieda turned to Uncle Louis, her voice spiced with Bavarian mischief. "Don't you want to see Sarah again? And reminisce about the good old days?"

There was a long pause while Uncle Louis weighed his options.

"No," he declared at last. "I don't want to embarrass the princess. Go ahead, Rudolf."

So Rudolf went alone.

The princess had brought her husband, the impressive-looking, tall and very elegant Prince Enesco. What a good thing Uncle Louis had stayed back-stage.

Not a word was said about the missed three o'clock appointment. Rudolf produced the tiara. The prince examined it carefully, nodded his approval, and reached for his wallet to hand him a hundred thousand marks in cash.

8

Shock Treatment

In 1926, Otto Koch was in Grade Two of the elementary Varrentrap Schule. His brother, Robert, was in Grade Three. Otto's teacher was Karl Beicht, whom he liked very much, as did most of the forty boys in his class. Later, at the Goethe Gymnasium, it was *de rigueur* to live in a permanent state of psychological warfare with the teachers. But Otto did not go there until 1929, when he was ten. At the Varrentrap Schule harmony prevailed.

Corporal punishment was rare. Only when heavily provoked would Herr Beicht ask a child to hold out his hands so that he could softly touch them with the wooden pointer he usually carried for symbolic reasons.

One day during a session on *Heimatkunde* — local geography — Otto dozed off. There was no rational explanation. He had had enough sleep and *Heimatkunde* was one of his favourite subjects. He always tried to please Herr Beicht. And he usually achieved a two plus (the equivalent of B plus) on his report card.

Herr Beicht noticed the sleeping boy, sitting in an aisle seat. So, as he walked up and down the aisle, while lecturing the class on the origins of the pink sandstone that gave many of Frankfurt's buildings their special character, Herr Beicht caressed him on the shoulder with his wooden pointer, without interrupting his discourse. Otto woke up and began sobbing, not screaming but sobbing.

Herr Beicht strolled back towards him.

"What's the matter, Koch?" he asked him gently. No one was ever addressed with his first name. "Aren't you feeling well?"

Instead of responding Otto went on sobbing.

"Would you like to go home?" Herr Beicht asked.

"Yes," Otto sobbed.

For the rest of the day Otto continued sobbing, off and on. When his mother and his governess, Fräulein Annelies, asked what was hurting him all he said was, "Herr Beicht hit me," which no one believed. He brushed off his kind-hearted and generous brother, when Robert suggested they play with their tin soldiers, even after he said Otto could pick Frederick the Great's soldiers in Prussian uniform, so Otto could beat Robert's French ones. Nothing could soothe him.

He slept well that night, but the next morning, stubbornly, he refused to go to school. His mother thought there was no point making a fuss about this and kept him at home. The following day Otto still refused to go. This time his mother decided to consult Herr Beicht. He was bound to have experience with this sort of situation. She went at ten thirty, at recess time.

They were in the school yard surrounding by yelling boys.

He told her what happened that morning in the classroom.

"I confess," she said, "I'm a bit worried about him."

"I agree it's puzzling. Who knows what goes on in the little boy's head?"

"I've been thinking of taking him away for a few days. Maybe to his grandmother's place in the Taunus, or somewhere in the Black Forest."

"I think that is unnecessary." Her Beicht said. "Take him to his doctor. Make him feel he is sick, as though he has a bit of the flu or a stomach ache. He's used to being cured by the doctor. I am sure the doctor will figure something out."

"That's a very useful idea, Herr Beicht," Otto's mother exclaimed. "I knew you'd come up with the right answer. I shall certainly follow your advice."

On the way home she wondered whether to call the family's pediatrician, Dr. Paul Grosser, or Dr. Richard Koch who was a kindred spirit as well as her late husband's cousin. But Otto had never been his patient. The trouble with both was that it was almost impossible to get their immediate attention. In Richard's case, there was another factor. When he was not teaching his course on the history of medicine at the university or lecturing at the *Jüdische Lehrhaus*, the Jewish Adult Education Institute, he was dealing with mostly serious cases in his private practice. Compared to these, Otto's condition was embarrassingly trivial.

Still, she decided Richard had the requisite degree of empathy and imagination. Also, he had been unusually fond of Otto's father, who had been two years younger.

But then she stopped in her tracks. Otto must have overheard many conversations at the dinner table about Richard's extraordinary friend and patient Franz Rosenzweig, whom she had also visited a few times. In the boy's mind, she thought, the association between Uncle Richard and a philosopher suffering from the final stages of ALS — amyotrophic lateral sclerosis, a progressive neurodegenerative disease — might scare him off. But she was prepared to ignore that, even though Otto must have heard that this great Jewish scholar was no longer able to move, to breathe without difficulty, to speak, to swallow normally, to write, to communicate with anybody except his wife, and only then with the help of a special machine. He must also have been puzzled by the frequent references — of course, far above the head of a six-year-old — to the profound book of philosophy Rosenzweig had scribbled on innumerable postcards and bits of paper in the trenches of Macedonia while he was a soldier on the Russian front. The book had been widely acclaimed as unique when it was published in 1921. It was imbued with the same spirit that made it possible for him later to bear his illness and the approach of death in a joyful, serene, even humorous way.

Otto's mother decided to risk it. When she phoned, Richard's wife, Maria, responded. She was his nurse and secretary. The clinic was on the ground floor of their house on the Savignystrasse.

"I'll tell you what to do, Ida," she said. "Come right away. I expect him home in about twenty minutes. Seeing you and Otto will be a pleasant surprise. Don't come to the clinic. The waiting room is full. Ring the bell at the front door."

Maria was right. Richard was delighted.

In less than thirty seconds Otto's mother gave him the facts.

Richard turned to Otto.

"Oh," he said, full of sympathy, "Herr Beicht certainly is a brute."

"He is not!" Otto replied.

"So why don't you want to go school?"

"I don't like it any more."

"Now, if you come with me to my clinic, I think I can make you like it again. What do you think of that?"

Otto swallowed a sob and nodded.

Richard led the way to the clinic through a back door, avoiding the waiting room. He made Otto sit on a chair, turned on a machine and quickly touched his hand with something like a toothbrush.

It gave him the mildest of electric shocks.

Otto could not wait to go to school the next morning and, thanks to Uncle Richard's magic touch, became an exemplary student ever after.

+++

In the fall of 1937 Richard Koch heard from friends with connections that only by leaving Germany within a few days could he be spared arrest. Maria rushed to Berlin, did the rounds of various embassies within a few hours and finally arranged with the Soviets to have him appointed immediately to a responsible medical position in Essentuki, a spa in the northern Caucasus. Richard was entirely unpolitical and did not speak Russian, but evidently emigration to no other country could have been arranged with comparable speed and no other country offered him a medical position of importance without having to take any exams. Two of their five children went with their parents. One daughter had already left for Palestine, the other for the United States.

The remaining twelve years of his life were extraordinarily productive. He found the work satisfying and was treated with the greatest respect. As far as anybody knows, he never uttered a word of criticism of the authorities. Until 1941, and again after the war, Richard carried on a voluminous correspondence with friends, old colleagues and relatives, among others Otto's mother. This helped him overcome his isolation from his family. His Russian remained elementary but in his last years he learned some Hebrew. He died in 1949 at the age of sixty-seven.

In the summer of 1942 Richard and Maria and their daughter, Gertrud, were evacuated to Georgia. (Their son Friedrich fought in the Red Army.) They survived under conditions of unbelievable hardship and deprivation, until the end of 1943 when they could return. Essentuki had been occupied by the Germans. Richard's library, mainly books of medical history, had disappeared, only to be discovered years later in Kishinev, the happy conclusion of a detective story that made a splash in the Soviet press.

While in Georgia he began writing his memoirs. This was not easy because whatever paper was available was in great demand as fuel for fire and to be used for smoking. However, he managed, and his wife and daughter later had the almost impossible task of deciphering his handwriting on the paper they had scrounged for him. What emerged was an extraordinarily detailed document, beautifully written: a cultural and medical history of the early twentieth century, an incredible feat of memory. A shortened version was published in Germany in 2004 by Frommann-Holzboog, edited by Frank Töpfer and Urban Wiesing.

On September 8 and 9, 1982, the University of Frankfurt held a seminar to examine Richard Koch's role as a doctor and, through his writing and teaching, as a precursor of holistic medicine.

+++

We did not find out until after the war that Karl Beicht, Otto's teacher in the Varrentrap Schule, was Jewish.

He perished in Auschwitz.

9

Social Research

On Saturday mornings the two Koch boys went to school but in the afternoon Fräulein Annelies occasionally took them to the Café Laumer on the Bockenheimer Landstrasse, corner Ulmenstrasse, for pastry. It was only three blocks north of the Rüsterstrasse. It so happened that the café was a favourite hangout of artists and academics, especially the faculty and students of the Institute for Social Research, which was affiliated with the nearby university. In fact, some seminars were held upstairs, a fact of no interest whatsoever to the Koch boys or their governess.

In the autumn of 1927 they went there one Saturday afternoon and found the boys' cousin Robert Heilbrunn sitting at a table with a beautiful girl named Gaby. Robert was Rudolf's younger brother, named like Otto's brother after grandfather Robert Koch. Rudolf was bookish and serious. By contrast Robert made a point of being non-bookish, a man-about-town who knew everybody, pleasure loving, amusing, the first person in his circle to join a golf club. At twenty-three he had just finished his legal studies in Heidelberg with distinction. His parents gave him plenty of play money while he was taking his time to decide whether to join his father in his law practice, follow his older brother at Robert Koch, or do something else, preferably nothing.

The smoke-filled place was crowded but a table for three had just been vacated next to Robert's, so he waved to them, pointed to it and they took it. Robert introduced them, complimented Annelies on her beautiful blond hair and asked the boys a few perfunctory questions about school. After that, the boys listened carefully to the conversation and, to their surprise, even understood some of it, although Otto's attention wandered a few times as he eyed the pastry on the counter, wondering whether Annelies would let him have another *Mohrenkopf,* the "moor's head" pastry with whipped cream covered with a chocolate roof.

"Do you see that man over there?" Robert asked Gaby, pointing to an unshaven man sitting at a table alone, a workingman's cap on his head, a cigarette hanging from his mouth, a half-emptied glass of beer in front of him.

"A Frenchman," Gaby ventured. "Or a Frankfurter who wants to look like a Frenchman."

"You guessed right the first time. His name is Fernand Gravin."

An elderly man, presumably a professor, approached Monsieur Gravin and asked him something. They both laughed. He looked familiar to the boys.

"That is a friend of your mother's, Franz Oppenheimer," Robert H explained.

"Oh yes," said Robert K. "We've met him. He's been to our place. He wrote a book and scribbled a few words on the first page, meant just for Ida Koch."

"He's a famous economist. Do you know what economists are?"

The boys shook their heads.

"They study money," Robert Heilbrunn explained. "Your mother is a beautiful rich widow. So naturally he is interested in her. But she turned him down."

Gaby laughed but the boys did not quite understand the joke. Annelies did and was not amused.

"What do you think he and the Frenchman were talking about?" Gaby asked.

"Oppenheimer probably asked him whether he was enjoying life in the bourgeoisie. And Gravin laughed and said 'not bad,' or something like that. Do you want to know how the Frenchman got to Frankfurt?"

Before Robert could tell Gaby, another man, this time younger and not so jovial, approached Monsieur Gravin.

"That is Jakob Becker," Robert explained. "He's a historian. Very nationalistic. His subject is the peasants' revolt. He tells everybody he's a friend of Hindenburg and that he doesn't like the Bauhaus or the Chosen People."

"Never mind him," Gaby said. "Tell me why Gravin is here."

Robert opened his mouth to answer, but suddenly a middle-aged man with glasses and a Berlin accent appeared at the table. "Heilbrunn, how come I always see you with a beautiful woman?"

Robert gave a little laugh. "This is Walter Benjamin," he said to Gaby. He introduced Benjamin to everyone at the table, and then turned back to Gaby. "As you can see, Walter is a shrewd judge of character. And a good friend of our uncle Richard." He smiled at Benjamin. "I just tried to tell Gaby the story of Fernand Gravin."

Benjamin laughed. "Yes, that's one of the few uplifting stories that have happened in this mixed-up university. It's like importing an unemployed Danish prince from Elsinore to explain *Hamlet*. *Au revoir.*"

"Now tell me," Gaby said after Benjamin had gone.

By now somebody else was talking to Fernand Gravin, and writing down every word he said on a pad of paper.

"About a month ago," Robert began, "a graduate student with the name of Joseph Dünner spent a few days in Paris. He has a scholarship and is a communist. Not the only communist in the Institute, as you can imagine. He's working on the French working class, following in the footsteps of Karl Marx, no doubt. In Paris, after a night's carousing with his comrades they went to a café near *Les Halles,* to have onion soup for breakfast. That's where Dünner met Gravin. They got talking. Gravin told him lurid stories about the exploited workers of Paris. So Dünner invited him to visit him in Frankfurt and said he would see to it that the university would pay for the trip and a hotel and all that. The French man agreed. Dünner told Horkheimer about him when he returned. He's the head of the department. He and his friend Teddy Adorno were so enchanted with the proposal that they decided to hire him for a month and give him an office. They encouraged all those who are working on the *Lumpenproletariat,* on thieves, tramps and prostitutes, and the underclass anywhere in the world, to consult him. They were all told to get their information from real life, instead of out of books. That's very much in the spirit of our Institute of Social Research. Oh, look who has just walked in — Paul Hindemith and Max Beckmann."

The composer and the painter sat down at a table not far from them and waved at Robert.

Gaby was more interested in Fernand Gravin.

"So, what happened?"

"One day at noon, somebody noticed that his overcoat was missing. And then several others discovered their wallets had vanished. But more importantly, some of the essays the students had written had disappeared. And so had Fernand Gravin. Presumably he intended to sell them to capitalist publishers, thinking they would pay him a fortune for them."

"Are you making this up, Robert?"

"Certainly not," Robert replied indignantly. "They decided not to call the police, but I assume with the help of high officials of the Communist Party, with which the Institute no doubt has excellent relations, they found him and persuaded him to return the stolen goods. He did so, obediently. And now, as you can see, the class struggle has been called off, at least temporarily, and Universal Love prevails."

+++

Franz Oppenheimer was the only economist ever to appear on a German stamp. His prize student was Ludwig Erhard, the father of the "Economic Miracle" and who followed Konrad Adenauer as chancellor and who attributed his success largely to Oppenheimer's free enterprise teachings. Oppenheimer died in Los Angeles in 1943.

In 1933 the Nazis closed down the Institute for Social Research, the home of The Frankfurt School of sociology. Some of the leading personalities immediately left Germany and became influential intellectuals in the United States.

+++

Robert Heilbrunn emigrated to London soon after 1933 and later to California, but remained undecided what to do with his life. During the war he worked as a stevedore in San Francisco and fruit picker in nearby orchards. After the war he was able to make use of his knowledge of German law: he worked for the U.S.

occupation in Bonn for several years in the area of decartelizing German industry. Soon after that came to an end, he suffered a collapse of some sort from which he never fully recovered. After many yeas of feuding with his family and living off his friends, he died in an old age home in the slums of Washington DC in 1991.

10

Nelly

In 1928 the *Intendant* of Radio Stuttgart gave a dinner in the *Schwäbische Turm* ostensibly to mark the twenty-fifth anniversary of Albert Meister's engagement as first cellist in the radio orchestra, but the real reason for the dinner had nothing to do with him. Rumours had been circulating that Nelly, the wife of my mother's younger brother, Emil Kahn, was becoming restless and wanted her husband to move on and become a fish in a bigger pond. Emil was Director of Music at the station and conductor of the orchestra. If he were to leave, it would be a serious loss, and a dinner of this sort would be good for the morale of the orchestra and an incentive for its conductor to resist his wife and stay.

The invitation specifically included Frau Kahn. She was rarely seen in public with her husband and was known to dislike dressing up for official functions. But she sometimes attended rehearsals and never missed any of his public concerts. The *Intendant's* secretary remarked to her boss that she probably did not even own a decent dress although, according to the station's personnel manager, her father was a university professor in Frankfurt and had considerable private means. (Emil Kahn, too, was listed as the son of a wealthy banker.) She added in the same catty tone that Nelly Kahn evidently enjoyed being pregnant. She had had four children in eight years, the last one only born a few weeks earlier. She was also said to be unusually superstitious and put people off because she had no interest in small talk. Nelly was apparently highly artistic, wrote poetry and painted, was interested in odd things and did not allow her children to play with any toys made in factories, only with toys made by nature — her house was full of pinecones — or by human hands. Also, she encouraged her children to eat spaghetti *au naturel* with their hands, on the assumption that they would learn to eat them the unnatural way soon enough.

The *Schwäbische Turm* was by no means Stuttgart's grandest hotel, but it was close to the radio station and housed many of its visitors. It also served perfectly satisfactory ceremonial dinners. For the Albert Meister dinner the menu consisted of minestrone, venison with red cabbage and *Spätzle*, and a banana pudding, all this to be washed down with a rather potent local red wine.

Everyone had sat down before Nelly arrived, fifteen minutes late, to her husband's acute embarrassment. He was punctilious about time — any player who was late for a rehearsal was publicly castigated. The other dinner guests, the men at any rate, forgave her quickly. Nelly Kahn turned out to be enchanting, a great beauty. None of the other ladies present could hold a candle to her and they all knew it. Petite, with an oval face and large expressive brown eyes, a perfect complexion and a *Bubikopf* — bangs — no one would have believed she was the mother of four children. She wore a simple red dress, with a very short skirt, no make-up and no jewellery, except for a simple wedding ring.

When she arrived all eyes turned to her. She stopped at the door, near the upright piano, not knowing to whom to apologize for her tardiness. Her husband discreetly pointed to the *Intendant*. She went to him. They shook hands. He was so impressed by her unexpected charms that he was about to ask her to forgive him, although he would not have known for what.

Nelly had been placed to the right of the guest of honour, Albert Meister. On her left was Horst Karlebach, the head of the *Abteilung Wort,* the Talks Department. Opposite her sat the *Intendant*. Emil Kahn was placed to the left of the *Intendant's* wife, Elsa, and to the right of Frau Ilse Meister.

Now, at last, everybody could begin the minestrone.

"I've always wondered," Albert Meister opened the conversation, "where your husband was trained as a conductor."

"In Leipzig," she responded. "He studied with Hermann Scherchen. Did you know he also plays the cello?"

"No," he replied. "He has never mentioned it."

"That's strange. As a matter of fact, he may be alive only because he plays the cello."

"What do you mean?" Albert Meister frowned heavily and scratched the back of his head. He was a big heavy man and a rather unpleasantly sour odour wafted towards her.

"In the last year of the war he was stationed in Alsace. Let me see ... he was twenty-one. He had joined up in 1915 when he was only eighteen. It so happened that his commanding officer loved chamber music. So the officer asked his sergeants to find out whether there was enough talent among his men to form a string quartet. There was. Paul Hindemith played the viola. We've been good friends ever since. I've often read his palm — he will become one of our best-known composers, that is absolutely certain. I don't remember who the others were. Naturally, the officer kept them out of harm's way so that he could listen to Mozart and Beethoven in peace whenever it suited him. Just before the end of the war we got married and I followed him to the front."

Everybody was listening, fascinated.

"You must have been a child, Frau Kahn," the *Intendant* said.

"I am two years younger. We were already soul partners as children. In Alsace, I was doing farm work nearby, so that my husband and I could meet occasionally in a barn and make love. During the day or night. I liked it best during the day. My husband is very good at it."

A number of soup spoons were suspended in mid air.

"Nelly." Her husband shook his head, half-smiling. "One does not talk about such things."

"Why not? Isn't it true? One can talk about anything if it's true."

Emil decided to change the subject. He asked the *Intendant's* wife whether she had heard about the amazing Berlin success of *Die Dreigroschenoper,* Kurt Weill and Bertold Brecht's The Beggar's Opera.

"Oh yes," the lady exclaimed. "Everybody's talking about it."

They continued discussing it for a few minutes until suddenly Nelly got up and went straight over to her husband and whispered something in his ear.

"Can I change seats with you right away? I cannot sit next to Albert Meister one moment longer. I know what he is thinking. Did you know he's a child molester?"

Emil shook his head vehemently.

"We can't do that!"

"In that case I'm leaving."

"Let me think."

He closed his eyes.

"You sit here," he said to Nelly, rising from his chair. "My wife suggests," he announced to the assembled guests, "that I should play something from the *Dreigroschenoper* on the piano. May I?"

"Oh please," everybody demanded.

Emil took his glass of wine and went to the piano. Accompanying himself he sang:

> *Und der Haifisch, der hat Zähne*
> *und die trägt er im Gesicht*
> *und Macheath, der hat ein Messer*
> *doch das Messer sieht man nicht.*
> [And the shark, he has teeth
> And he wears them in his face
> And MacHeath, he has a knife
> But the knife you do not see.]

He then added his own *specialité*. He announced, "Now let me play this the way Mozart would have written it." And he did so, to the delight of everybody. Ditto, Beethoven and Wagner. Then he returned to the table and sat down next to Albert Meister, without a single word to explain the change of seats. The conversation resumed as though the seating was the same as before.

"Somebody mentioned to me the other day," said Horst Karlebach, the head of the *Abteilung Wort,* to Nelly across the table, "that you are related to the economist Siegfried Budge."

"I am his only child," Nelly replied proudly.

"Oh really? We've broadcast a lecture of his in which he criticized Franz Oppenheimer rather severely."

"Yes, but they are good friends. I have analyzed the handwriting of both, you know, and I could immediately see that they're brothers at heart. My father's book about him is called *Der Kapitalprofit: Eine kritische Untersuchung unter besonderer Berücksichtigung der Theorie Franz Oppenheimers* [A Critical Examination of Capital Profit with Special Reference to Franz Oppenheimer's Theory]. He published it nearly ten years ago, just after the war. I don't understand a word of it. Nor does he understand my path of spiritual training to acquire continuity of consciousness."

Horst Karlebach took this last bit in his stride.

"Did you see a lot of him when you were growing up?"

"No, he was always too busy. I was brought up like a princess. My governess even took me to school every day, until I rebelled. I think I was fifteen. By then I was old enough to understand, without her help, or my mother's, that people did not wish to hear the plain, unvarnished truth because it is usually uncomfortable. I also soon discovered that neither of them could compete with Goethe and Schiller to help me cope with my sexual awakening."

The *Intendant* saved Karlebach from the need to comment on this discovery.

"Frau Kahn, do you usually agree with your husband's musical interpretations?"

"I do," Nelly replied, gravely. "I think he's a great musician. Very sensitive. But there is only one thing wrong."

"And that is?"

"He understands perfectly well that when we hear music we all feel that it harmonizes with what we experience in our inner selves. But he has not yet developed the faculty to perceive tone combinations and varieties of tone inaudible to the physical ear. And in order for him to be able to do that, he needs to train himself to manage, as I do, with only four hours sleep a night. He still sleeps for six, seven hours."

"Are you serious, Frau Kahn?" The *Intendant* could not believe his ears. "You only sleep for four hours every night?"

"My friend tells me to cut it down to two," Nelly responded.

+++

Two weeks after the dinner Albert Meister was arrested for sexual offences committed in a park with several young boys.

A short time later Nelly left her husband to follow a friend who, like her, was a follower of Rudolf Steiner. Nelly and Emil agreed to divorce. She suggested that he marry one of his singing students, Ellen Beck, which he did. Nelly and her friend left Stuttgart. Two or three years later her parents were notified that she had been admitted to a mental institution in Berlin and diagnosed as a schizophrenic. She died in the mid 'thirties.

Emil lost his job as soon as the Nazis came to power in 1933 and went to New York alone, leaving his second wife and three of the four children in her care, to follow later. The youngest child, Wolf, was taken to Frankfurt, to be brought up by his grandmother Kahn until he was ready to leave.

Nelly's father, Siegfried Budge, died of natural causes in 1941. Her mother, Ella, perished in Theresienstadt.

11

The Magic Mountain

When Emil Netter was discharged from the Merkur-Sanatorium in Davos in 1924, after a sojourn of ten years as a tuberculosis patient, the director, Dr. Egon Gellert, asked him to promise him to remain in touch and, above all, to consult him whenever he was facing a major decision. Five years later, in October 1929, Netter visited him, for the first time since he left, to introduce to him the woman he intended to marry: Ida Koch, Otto's mother.

Tall, imposing, completely bald, often wearing a monocle, highly articulate, Emil Netter was thirty-seven, two years younger than Ida Koch. He was one of the partners of Wolf Netter und Jakobi, manufacturers of corrugated iron, with several plants in southern and western Germany. The company, founded by his grandfather, was a major element of the German steel industry.

Emil Netter was born in Strasbourg. His father and grandfather had been natives of Bühl, in the Black Forest near Baden-Baden, just the other side of the Rhine. That is the small town where the company was founded. Bühl was also the birthplace of Ida Koch's mother, Anna Kahn. There was therefore an affinity between the two families. After 1870, when Alsace became German, the Netters transferred their headquarters to its capital. In 1918–19, when Strasbourg became French again, the family had to leave, like the other German Jews who had come to Alsace since 1870. The Netters went to Frankfurt and Berlin.

Dr. Egon Gellert was in his late fifties, white haired and pink cheeked, with bags under his eyes. He welcomed Netter and his fiancée.

The three of them had made themselves comfortable in easy chairs in a corner of the director's office, around a table dominated by a vase of dark blue mountain flowers.

Dr. Gellert
Frau Koch, I hope your friend has told you that once a man has been my patient for one day he remains my patient for life. If he's been mine for ten years, he's mine for eternity. With women, even longer.

Emil Netter (to Ida Koch)
This doctor is power-mad.

Ida Koch
I can see that.
(Laughter.)

Dr. Gellert
You two have made the pilgrimage to Davos to ask for my blessing. I've always regarded my role as a doctor primarily to be that of a cleric. But I withhold my blessing far more frequently than most clerics do. Do you know what you two are doing? (To Ida:) Let me describe your friend to you.

Emil Netter
No, no, no. Don't do that, Dr. Gellert. Let me first describe Ida Koch to you.

Dr. Gellert
Go ahead.

Emil Netter
Ida Koch is far more than a beautiful woman of the world. Her father was a banker and her husband a jeweller, but she has no use for the shallow charms of material glitter. She prefers, as I do, the non-material things that matter. That is very rare among people with her background, even though on her mother's side there is a strong artistic streak. In fact, she's a little too frugal for my liking, but I intend to cure her of that. One thing I like about her is that she has a logical mind and is entirely unsentimental. She is also a splendid mother and knows how to instruct her cook not to overdo the vegetables. Fate cheated her out of a good first marriage, first, by taking her husband away to war for four years, after they had been married for only a short time and had one daughter, and then by removing him from this earth altogether, for no apparent

reason, only one year after his return from the battlefield. She may not deserve what I have to offer, but you will have to agree that she has a right to a new beginning.

Dr. Gellert
A very lucid testimonial, Herr Netter. Do you have anything to add, Frau Koch?

Ida Koch
Only that I am grateful to Emil for bringing me here, to meet you and to show me the place where ...

Dr. Gellert
He was my patient for ten years. He was near death more than once. His youngest sister, Helen, could not be saved. She died while he was here. At twenty-four. (Pause.) That happened in 1923, I think.

Emil Netter
1922.

Dr. Gellert
His other sister had already succumbed in Berlin in 1915 — after his second year with us. She was just twenty. All three Netter children had been infected with tuberculosis. Who knows by whom. Members of a family that had enjoyed all the amenities that money can buy. Fate had removed two out of three.

Ida Koch
I know, I know.

Dr. Gellert
And here he is — the very picture of health and vitality, a captain of industry and no doubt the terrifying master of — how many hundreds of employees?

Emil Netter
Dr. Gellert, you have a very curious idea of what the world is like, down in the valley.

Dr. Gellert
I remember very well that you used to say only what happened down in the valley was serious. Up here, even removing the dead in the middle of the night through the back door, you'd

say was merely some sort of metaphysical theatre staged for no other purpose but to entertain me. Frau Koch, will you be able to live with a man who says such absurd things?

Ida Koch

I am looking forward to trying.

Emil Netter

Dr. Gellert, how can one live without absurdities? Every one of us is dealing with them all the time. After all, it's absurd that the questions we find most interesting are invariably insoluble. And that our aims are unattainable. And that our rational behaviour is almost always checkmated by the irrational. And that we're not only afraid of the irrational — that goes without saying — but we also have reverence for it. If that isn't absurd I don't know is.

Dr. Gellert

I am not surprised that your illness, ten years in the mountain air, reading books, writing letters and essays, and having endlessly profound philosophical conversations have robbed you of any illusions you may have had before coming here. And have given you the strength to face life with new ideas and many friends but without illusions.

Ida Koch

Yes, that is what I wanted to hear from you, Dr. Gellert, that he has the strength. He does, doesn't he?

Emil Netter

I have the strength to make a commitment. I did not have the strength to do so to the women I loved here.

Dr. Gellert

That is outside my jurisdiction.

Emil Netter

Not entirely. Nothing is outside a cleric's jurisdiction.

Dr. Gellert

All I need to know to assess your chances is that you both understand the risks you are taking. Doctors avoid the word "normal," but you must both realize that anything like a normal life after spending a third of it — please don't correct my arithmetic — in this magic no-man's-land, having suffered grave and lasting damage to your physical organism, Herr Netter, having earth-shattering love affairs on the edge of the grave while down in the valley there was a world war, a Russian revolution, a German revolution, Versailles, inflation, the Weimar Republic — no, I think that is impossible. It is asking for too much. Normalcy is out. Have you seen the newspapers this week?

Emil Netter
A stock exchange crash in New York. The president is saying everything will be back to normal in no time. I didn't know Swiss doctors were paying attention to such things.

Dr. Gellert
This one does. He needs it to assess the strength of others.

Ida Koch
Dr. Gellert, Emil has the strength to assume his share of responsibility running a major enterprise in a country that is at last slowly recovering from chaos.

Emil Netter
You mean, the strength to deal with my partners. That indeed requires superhuman strength!

Ida Koch (laughing)
That is not what I meant at all.

Dr. Gellert
Yes, but has he the strength also to become a stepfather? Of a girl of seventeen, of two boys, aged eleven and ten?

Emil Netter
They like me and I like them. They are at the top of my reasons for wanting to make the commitment.

Dr. Gellert
Good. The time has come for my verdict. Herr Netter, Frau Koch, go ahead. I don't only approve; I am delighted. No one who has not been through what you have been through, Herr Netter, can conceivably understand the joy, the triumph, of

merely being alive the way you do. I understand it — it is my business to understand it. And, Frau Koch, if any woman can help a great survivor like Herr Netter face the future I think you are. But you, too, must not have any illusions. Only because he looks so strong and vigorous, does not mean he is. This is very deceptive. He has been greatly weakened by illness. No one is ever completely cured. He has to avoid strains and excitements. He will be a difficult, moody, perhaps even choleric husband. You must understand that. You must give him priority, not over your children — he would not demand that — but over all your previous obligations. That is asking for a great deal. I am sure you understand.

Ida Koch
I do.

Dr. Gellert
Then, *bon voyage*! But remember — I shall always remain in charge!

+++

On the morning of February 9, 1936, Emil Netter shot himself in his office in Frankfurt, one of many Jews who committed suicide at that time. He lacked the strength to decide whether to emigrate to Palestine or to France. The marriage had been deteriorating for three years.

He was buried in Strasbourg.

12

The Twilight Bride

Letter from Dr. Maria Sinding to her friend and fellow alumna of the University of Frankfurt, Dr. Lore Heilbrunn, née Grages, on the occasion of Lore's wedding to Dr. Rudolf Heilbrunn, Otto Koch's cousin, on January 12, 1933, less than three weeks before Hitler came to power.

Dear Lore,

I can't tell you how much I enjoyed meeting your new in-laws. What an impressive family! As you know, I had met Rudolf before and liked him immensely. You chose well! When you introduced me to him just after your engagement in the intermission at the Neue Theater — was it the new Hauptmann play or Pygmalion? — I thought he was a professor of history, or maybe an editorial writer at the Frankfurter Zeitung. But a jeweller? Well, if one has to made a living it might as well be selling beautiful things to the *anciens riches* and the *nouveaux riches* in an establishment universally known as first class. I think it is safe to assume that your husband is the only collector of first editions of Spinoza engaged in this activity, anywhere in the world.

I don't know where to start. Did I like the grandmother best, the quintessential Old Frankfurter? She lost a husband and two sons and still has the vitality and good humour of a woman who's never had a bad day in her life. I was so amused when she said that she was demonstrating how you could have a good long life without having a cold bath every morning, something her mother had done all her life. That's why she lived until she was ninety-five! I was also enthralled by the story of her flight from

Frankfurt to the Taunus Mountains in 1866, when she was
seven and Bismarck's Prussians marched in to put an end
to Frankfurt's status as a Free City. Her mother had sewn
seven silver spoons into the hem of her skirts to keep them
from the greedy Prussians! "That is when all our troubles
started," she said, "when Bismarck took Frankfurt."

Or was I even more attracted by Rudolf's parents, Claire
Heilbrunn, a rock of grassroots common sense, and Justizrat
Dr. Ludwig Heilbrunn, the lawyer and former politician, a
model of civic-minded humanism, also the author of the
amusing verses Rudolf's teenage cousins Robert and Otto
had to recite, proudly celebrating the new addition to the
family, you, "Lore, the great Fontane scholar!" And all those
anecdotes about the fabulous "Onkel Louis," who died three
years ago and was still conducting the Koch orchestra from
the Beyond! I could have done without twelve-year-old Otto
playing the Mozart E minor violin sonata so dreadfully out
of tune, with his mother at the piano flinching from time
to time, but one has to take the rough with the smooth. His
older and wiser brother had the good sense to stay out of the
room while this was going on.

And then there was the other Robert, Rudolf's good-
looking younger brother, advertising the joys of being
single, sardonic, rich and slightly mysterious, clearly the
apple of his mother's eye. I wondered how those two
were getting along and whether a well-connected, name-
dropping young man could manage on his mother's love
forever. Now, please don't tell me that for symmetrical
reasons I should marry him. I won't. You know perfectly
well that I need somebody solid, down to earth, humble
and reliable. As a matter of fact, I have my eyes fixed
on the shoemaker at the corner of the Fahrgasse and
Dominikanerstrasse in the Old Town. I know he needs me
and I need to feel needed.

Now at last you can put to good use the many years
you spent analyzing those Theodor Fontane novels. You
won't be able to help looking at that family with his eyes,

using his social barometer and remembering, above all, his interest in Jewish matters and his many friendships with Jews. You will recall his changing views on the subject, from being very pro-Jewish as a young man, to being more — shall we say — detached about Jews in old age, at the end of the century, when he became increasingly doubtful whether the Jews as a group would ever be able to assimilate successfully to the Germans, as his own ancestors the Huguenots had. And he put the onus on the Jews, not on the Germans. Was that fair?

It would have done Fontane good to meet the Heilbrunn-Kochs. If any family is ripe for assimilation, they are. They certainly deserve it. There is not the slightest reason why Christian society should hesitate for one minute to welcome them with open arms. Any unseen observer listening to their conversation at the party I attended would not have been able to register a single discordant note to which a patriotic German might take exception. And the casualties the family suffered in the war were no less numerous than those in many of our families. They paid the price. For their ripeness for assimilation there is one simple proof — their delight in having you in the family, a child of the old Christian business elite. They were celebrating the first so-called "mixed marriage" in their history — no doubt the first of many to come. No wonder they celebrated in grand style. They have arrived! I bet you any money that, other things being equal, those young cousins of Rudolf, Robert and Otto, will also marry Christians. They are on their way!

A good thing the Nazis lost so many seats in the November election. It seems to me highly unlikely that they can recover and reverse the trend. Once the upward curve is broken, that's it. So we all, not only the Jews, have every right to breathe a huge sigh of relief. The worst is over.

Thanks again for inviting me to that lovely gathering.

Let's keep in touch.

Maria

+++

Letter from Dr. Lore Heilbrunn, to Dr. Maria Sinding, dated January 2, 1934.

Dear Maria,

Why, of all places, did you accept a teaching position in Magdeburg? I need you here near me. Please do something dreadful so they will throw you out.

You ask what I have to say about my first year as a married woman. Yes, in ten days we will observe our first anniversary. Well, I have only good things to say about Rudolf. He is a good argument for marriage. Behind that thinker's face and the philosophical and often ironic language — when he is not selling diamonds and pearls — there is an amazing conviction that the Nazis will not last, that the "Revolution will eat her children." That is what I am told they used to say in the French revolution. Those gangsters will destroy each other, he says, and the republic will ultimately be saved by the army. He is far more optimistic than I am, but he has a better political mind and is much better informed.

I have not told him that I had a letter from one of my uncles — not my favourite uncle, who is the international lawyer — suggesting with grossly misguided delicacy that the time may be approaching when I should consider it a service to our family to part ways from a husband who, in times like these, was a liability. I dismissed this suggestion in words far less delicate than his.

But I knew this sort of thing was coming when I saw a heavy-jawed storm trooper outside the Koch store on April 1, the day of the anti-Jewish boycott. Rudolf was in the store, and so were his partners and employees. A niece of the former grand duchess of Hesse said "Excuse me" as she pushed the storm trooper aside and went in. She said she was totally impoverished and couldn't buy anything but she wanted to make a point.

Soon after that Rudolf's beloved grandmother suffered
a terrible shock when Lilli Grosser, the woman who was
to marry her son Max, who was killed at the front in 1918,
announced that she and her husband were emigrating
to France. The husband was the pediatrician Dr. Paul
Grosser, who had been dismissed from his hospital within
a month after Hitler assumed power. Grandmother Koch
still felt Lilli was her daughter-in-law, in spite of the new
husband. She could not understand their departure at all.
She never recovered. You may note that Dr. Grosser took
a view diametrically opposite Rudolf's. Dr. Grosser thinks
the Nazis are just at their beginning. All Jews who could,
should leave as soon as possible.

Yes, that was no doubt the last blow in Grandmother
Koch's life. On November 18 she died, on the day of her
granddaughter Margo's twenty-first birthday. She had
been looking forward so much to the celebration. She was
seventy-four. I don't know how to explain this — but I felt
as though it had been my own grandmother who had died
— I dissolved in tears when I heard about it. The obsequies
in the Jewish cemetery to which she had gone every Friday
of her life, winter and summer, since her husband died
in 1902, were so sad, so terribly, terribly sad — tears are
welling up even as I think of them. Everybody, including
her chauffeur and her gardener, is still in deep mourning,
feeling that an era has come to an end.

Please visit us as soon as you can.

Lore

+++

In 1938 Rudolf Heilbrunn negotiated the sale of Robert Koch
under duress, its "Aryanization," at a fraction of its value for
currency that could not be taken out of Germany. He and Lore
emigrated to Holland, where he made a meager living in the rare
book business. On December 11th, 1942, he was arrested and sent
to the concentration camp of Westermark. There he managed to
write his autobiography, *Zehn Nachtwachen* [Ten Vigils], which

was published in 2000. From Westermark Anna Frank and many others were deported to Bergen-Belsen or Auschwitz, but Rudolf escaped deportation and was released, possibly thanks to Lore's connections, after ten months. The marriage did not survive the postwar period. He later returned to Germany in 1962 and, after a successful second marriage, died in Kaiserslautern in 1998, at the age of ninety-seven. Lore had died in Switzerland two years earlier. Although her family was in Germany, she never returned. She had not remarried.

13

Antigone

Ida Netter sat on the edge of her bed trying to decide what to wear. It was October 1934, too early for winter clothes. Later, when it got cold, it would not matter — she could wear anything under her fur coat. But it was too early for that — and a fur coat would have been wrong in any case. On this occasion it would be a mistake to play the role of the great lady. Much wiser to wear modest clothes and modest jewellery, perhaps only a silver bracelet — or none at all. And certainly no earrings.

Ida Netter was facing a difficult mission. Her husband, Emil, had encouraged her to make an appointment to see Dr. Eichhorn, the new principal of the *humanistische* Goethe Gymnasium, her sons' high school, which had a great liberal tradition. Students had to take French in the first year, Latin in the third, Greek in the fifth and no English unless they opted for it in the final two years, plus there was a heavy emphasis on history and the liberal arts. The new man, reputed to be an *Edelnazi* — a sarcastic term for a member of what the Nazis considered their social or intellectual nobility — had taken the place of Dr. Ernst Neustadt, who had been dismissed, together with all other Jews in the public service, on October 1, 1933, as a result of the *Gesetz zur Wiederherstellung der Berufsbeamtentums* [Law for the Restoration of the Professional Civil Service]. Dr. Neustadt was an eminent classical scholar and a universally respected pedagogue.

The Goethe Gymnasium was said to be under the special protection of one of its old boys, Prince Philipp of Hesse, the *Oberpräsident* of Hessen-Nassau, a great grandson of Queen Victoria and the son-in-law of the king of Italy. He may well have had a say in the decision who was to be in charge of his alma mater.

Emil Netter had suggested this wife complain to Dr. Eichhorn about a disturbing incident involving her younger son, Otto. Now fifteen, he had come home from school recently with a torn shirt and a bruise on his left cheek. On cross-examination he had reluctantly told his mother that he had been in a fight with two other boys, in the changing room after gym. He had mentioned to her a week or two earlier that those two classmates, with whom he had always been on amicable terms, had just joined the Hitler Youth. Otto had insisted that it was a friendly fight — just routine *joie de vivre*. From the way he behaved Ida Netter suspected something ugly.

It would be instructive to meet the new headmaster, in any case, and obtain a first-hand impression of the new man. Of forty boys in Otto's class, eight were Jewish. Two had emigrated last spring: one had gone with his parents to Italy, the other had departed for the United States. Since the boycott of Jewish stores on April 1st last year and the legislation of October 1st, it had become increasingly unclear what the government's intentions were. Ida Netter was painfully torn between her new husband's acute and ever-increasing pessimism and the feeling shared by her first husband's relatives, the Heilbrunns, that this government of criminals could not last much longer. "The soup," they said, "was never eaten as hot as it was cooked."

At last, Ida Netter made her decision. She would wear a simple brown no-nonsense dress under her grey *Übergangsmantel* — her overcoat for in-between seasons.

As she was walking down the Rheinstrasse towards the school, along the same *Schulweg* her sons walked daily to school, she pondered what membership in the Hitler Youth really meant in the context of the Goethe Gymnasium. It was customary for young people in all schools to belong to a youth group if they so chose. The Hitler Youth was one of these. Young Jews belonged to the *Werkleute* (the Zionist group) or the *Blaue Fähnlein* (the non-Zionist group). Robert was thinking of joining the *Werkleute*. No doubt he was influenced by Emil Netter's interest in Zionism. Emil regularly sent installments of his large library, assembled over ten years spent in Davos, to the Hebrew University in Jerusalem, which relied on such contributions.

Before January 1933, each political party had its own youth group, which wore one of several colours of shirts, a red shirt or a brown shirt, among others, and was identified by various types of insignia. They all had certain activities in common, such as camping and singing songs around a fire. Naturally, there was the odd comparing of notes about common denominators such as the best type of canvas for tents. Even after Hitler's assumption of power such non-ideological information was still being exchanged between members of the Hitler Youth and the Jewish campers. After all, they also sat together in class and did their exercises together in the gym.

To Ida Netter's relief no swastika flag had been hoisted in front of the school. This was being done throughout the city more and more frequently, on all kinds of occasions. But fortunately not here today. She could read the Latin inscription under the upstairs windows undisturbed: VITAE NON SCHOLAE DISCIMUS — we learn for life, not for the school — a mission statement, of course, vigorously disputed by the boys. The normal condition between them and their teachers was one of constant mutual warfare. Rarely was a cordial relationship between any one teacher and any one boy publicly admitted.

As Ida Netter was walking up the stairs and along the corridors towards the principal's office, passing the portraits of Socrates, Plato, Cicero, Caesar and Marcus Aurelius, a number of older boys rushed past her on their way to the *Aula*, the assembly hall. She stopped a young student who was walking in the opposite direction and asked him what was going on.

"The dress rehearsal for *Antigone*," the boy responded. "For tonight's performance." He looked at his watch. "They're five minutes late." He added with a laugh, "Good thing the *Wutz* isn't in charge."

Many teachers had nicknames, not necessarily malicious. *Wutz* — vernacular for pig — was merely a play on the name of Dr. Wirtz, a stickler for punctuality. Others, like *Schwalch,* owed their nicknames to far-fetched or forgotten origins and were chosen because they sounded right. On the other hand, *Lieschen* for Dr. Weber was obvious because of his prissy, slightly effeminate manner. With few exceptions, the pre-Nazi teachers in the Goethe Gymnasium were eminent scholars with qualifications comparable with those of university professors. The *Oberprima* — the senior class leading to the *Abitur,* the final exam — was in some ways equivalent to first-year university.

The principal's secretary kept Ida Netter waiting for only ten minutes. She spent the time trying to remember what *Antigone* was about. Wasn't that the story of the brave daughter of Oedipus who defied the tyrant Creon and, against his orders, insisted on burying her rebellious brother, and paid for it with her death? The gods were on the side of the rebels, she remembered, not of the tyrant. She wondered what the Nazi teachers would make of the play. And, by the way, would they have a boy play Antigone?

At last the door opened and Dr. Eichhorn, a little silver swastika in his lapel, stepped out to greet her. He exuded an aroma of eau de cologne. In his late thirties, handsome and athletic, he did not look at all unpleasant. By showing her into his office and offering her a chair in an extravagantly polite and respectful manner, he evidently wanted to indicate that, whatever she may have heard about him, he knew how to behave. No doubt he had informed himself that Frau Netter was the mother of the two Jewish Koch boys in his school and he wanted to demonstrate to her that he wasn't a goon.

"My secretary informs me, *gnädige Frau,*" he opened the conversation, "that you wanted to see me in connection with an incident involving your younger son, Otto Koch. He is in the *Untersekunda,* isn't he?" *"Gnädige Frau"* was a polite, old-fashioned, upper-class form of address.

"Yes, that is right," Otto's mother said. "But before we talk about it, may I congratulate you on the choice of the play for the performance tonight. I just found out about it. I think that is very enterprising of you."

"Thank you, *gnädige Frau,*" he replied. "I am very proud that our school still does performances of plays in classical Greek."

"Oh, I had not thought of that." Ida Netter was duly impressed. "You are really doing it in Greek?"

"Oh yes," he laughed. "This is probably the last year. I doubt whether our *Gauleiter* will get much pleasure from it. But he isn't in charge of the curriculum yet. Still..."

"When I said it was enterprising of you," Ida Netter chose her words carefully, "I was really thinking of something else. I was wondering how the teachers would interpret the play without running afoul of some of the new thinking."

"I don't know what you mean," he said with surprising sharpness. Of course Dr. Eichhorn knew exactly what she meant.

"I mean the heroine is very much opposed to authority. I would have thought this might create certain difficulties."

Dr. Eichhorn leaned back in his chair.

"Frau Netter" — no longer *gnädige Frau* — "if I may say so, I think your understanding of the approach to these matters is gravely flawed, both to the play and to the 'new thinking.' Sophocles did not write the play to undermine authority. It would hardly have lasted two and half thousand years if he had. It is a play about character, about the formation of character in adversity. This is entirely in line with what you call the new thinking. We believe that the primary purpose of education is the formation of character. We have seen what the overemphasis on rational thinking and intellectualizing has led to — indecision, softness and effete decadence. Now please tell me about the incident involving your son. How can I help you?"

This is by no means going well, Ida Netter thought to herself. "Before I tell you about it, Dr. Eichhorn, I must inform you that this is the first time I have called on any teacher, or school authority, in a matter of this sort. I would not want to waste their time complaining about trivia. My family has had a long connection with the Goethe Gymnasium. Both my brothers attended."

"I'm afraid I did not have that privilege," Dr. Eichhorn responded tartly. "I come from a small town near Koblenz. You mention 'a matter of this sort'. Of what sort, may I ask?"

She told him about the fight in the changing room, without mentioned the Hitler Youth. All she said was "two against one." She did not wish to suggest, she said, that Herr Jansen, the teacher in charge, was aware of it or that he should have been aware of such a minor incident. No doubt such fights among adolescent boys occurred all the time. But from the way Otto talked about it she had the strong impression that there had been — here she hesitated — political overtones. Of course, she may have been wrong about this. She wanted to add that Otto had not wanted her to come here and that she had not told him she was coming.

"I see." Dr. Eichhorn inspected his fingernails. "I understand you perfectly. You need go no further. All I can say is that you will have to expect more and more incidents of this sort."

"I do?" she asked. "Jewish children are admitted to the schools, like everybody else. Jews pay taxes. How can you justify hooliganism on school premises?"

"Once again, Frau Netter, you misunderstand. I certainly do not 'justify any hooliganism,' to use your words. All I am saying is that you must expect it. Boys have instincts, as well as reasoning powers. On many occasions instincts are more important. Boys instinctively react against other boys who are fundamentally different from them."

Ida Netter was aghast.

"I don't think," she said helplessly, "any school principal in my brothers' days in the Goethe Gymnasium would have said that."

"That is no doubt true." Dr. Eichhorn looked at his watch. "Naturally. They would not have had the scientific knowledge about racial differences that we impart in our biology classes."

He rose in his chair and bowed to her.

"Thank you very much, *gnädige Frau,* for coming to see me."

On the way out she had to make her way through a crowd of boys coming out of the *Aula,* where the dress rehearsal had just concluded.

Ida Netter stopped one of the boys and asked who was playing Antigone.

"The one over there." The boy pointed to a handsome young man, probably in the *Oberprima.* She hoped he would have a shave before the performance tonight.

On his arm he was carrying the brown shirt he had worn earlier in the day at a meeting of the Hitler Youth.

He was humming the current hit, *Heute gehört uns Deurschland, morgen die ganze Welt* [Today We Own Germany, Tomorrow the Whole World].

14

Pop

The Master of Cornwallis House, C.H.C. Osborne, universally known as Pop, told Otto when he left Cranbrook School, Kent, in the spring of 1937, that he had been the worst house prefect since the founding of the public — that is, privately run — school by Queen Elizabeth in 1574. True, Pop was a historian, but how could he possibly have known? No, at best this was a gross exaggeration. When Otto had arrived two school years earlier, in the autumn of 1935, having spent the spring and summer with the family of a Methodist clergyman in Croydon to learn basic English, he did not have the slightest idea what a house prefect was, or that Cornwallis House was one of four constituent houses in Cranbrook School.

Traditionally, a house prefect is a senior boy responsible for the enforcement of certain rules. He is entitled to cane non-prefects who had broken one or more of these rules, such as the rule that there were certain doors only prefects were allowed to open and certain lawns only prefects were allowed to cross. He also has the services of a fag, a junior boy, to perform menial services, such as having his shoes shined. In his day, Winston Churchill was a fag at Harrow.

Pop made the observation about Otto's imperfect performance to make light of his own efforts to anglicize this fifteen-year-old refugee in whom he had taken a special interest. As a progressive Fabian socialist, he was pleased that Otto had never made use of his caning privilege but disappointed that he had remained incapable of learning what cricket was about. However, Pop appreciated the boy's valiant efforts since he realized that learning how to fake being an Englishman was an invaluable part of any foreigner's education. So Pop knew the time on the playing fields was not wasted.

Immediately after Ida Netter had reported to her husband the gist of her conversation with Otto's Nazi principal, they agreed that the boy must leave the school at the end of the year and, if possible, depart from Germany altogether. England seemed the obvious choice. Emil Netter consulted a friend who recommended Cranbrook School. Money for this was found outside Germany. As soon as Otto had finished the year his parents took him to London, spent three days with him in the Park Lane Hotel on Piccadilly and then delivered him to the family in Croydon.

No one could have invented a character more precisely the opposite of the Nazi principal than Pop. He was a dwarf, a highly intellectual dwarf who was a formidable teacher and housemaster, with a huge head — the head of Punch, with pink apple-cheeks — resting on a pathetically underdeveloped body. In Germany, even before the Nazis, it would have been difficult to imagine this miniature version of a human being commanding the affectionate respect of growing boys. Nothing endeared England as much to Otto as the spectacular phenomenon of Pop.

To his schoolmates, Otto was a puzzling phenomenon. What were they to make of a boy who kept a German sausage in his tuck box?

At Easter 1935, Hermann Goering married the actress Emmy Sonnemann. This wedding, attended by more than four hundred glittering dignitaries, received a great deal of publicity in the English papers, The boys remembered it in the autumn when Otto arrived. One of the them posed him this test question:

"Were your parents invited to the wedding?"

"No."

"Why not?"

"They did not qualify."

"Didn't they have enough pull?"

"It's not question of pull." For a number of good reasons Otto did not want to say "because they are Jewish." One reason was that the questioner would probably have asked 'What does *that* have to do with it?' "Even if they had qualified," Otto explained, "they would not have wanted to be invited. They don't think Goering is a nice man."

"Oh," the boy said, "he looks to me like a very jolly chap. Likes hunting and shooting. Can't be so bad. It's just sour grapes."

This Otto did not understand. So he let it go.

On another occasion there was a discussion at breakfast of a speech by Hitler assuring the world that he did not have the slightest desire to conquer other countries and that he wanted peace and nothing but peace.

Otto said, "Don't you believe it."

"So you want another war?" a boy asked.

"I certainly don't," Otto replied.

"My dad says," the boy cut him off, "the French are our enemies and not the Germans. Please pass me the porridge."

If there had been the slightest evidence of anti-Semitism at Cranbrook Pop would have gone to the greatest length to stamp it out. But Otto was convinced Pop understood there was no need for such counter-measures. Before Otto the boys had never met any Jews and most of them had never heard of any, except, of course, in the Bible, which had nothing to do with the real world. When Pop managed to excuse Otto from attending chapel in his second year, on the grounds that he was Jewish, many of the boys wanted to convert immediately.

If there was no prejudice against Jews there certainly was a prejudice against people with "brains."

"You're quite brainy, aren't you?" a boy asked one day.

Otto did not understand the question. Nobody had accused him of that in Frankfurt. It was his brother Robert who always had his nose in a book. So he vehemently denied it. He was, however, amazed when his first end-of-term report came out. It was far better than his reports had been at the Goethe Gymnasium and convinced him that the English had very peculiar standards. Perhaps brains weren't required to run the Empire, a skill supposed to be honed at schools like Cranbrook. (Pop was an anti-imperialist. But he was odd in every respect.) Some of the boys had only the vaguest ideas of what their fathers did for a living. They hardly knew them because they were stationed in distant parts of the Empire. The boys spent their holidays with various relatives. One of them astounded Otto when he mentioned that he only saw his father once every three years.

Was Otto given a good report because, as a result of his German conditioning, he paid more attention to classroom studies than the English? The reason why the boy asked whether he was brainy may have been because Otto was bad at games and was presumed to have *some* compensating qualities.

His modest ability to play the violin certainly impressed nobody. Instruments were not being taught at Cranbrook. However, the headmaster also happened to play the violin, much better than Otto did. On one occasion he was invited to his house to play Bach's Double Concerto with him, with the headmaster's wife at the piano. Soon afterward the headmaster mentioned to the headmistress of Benenden School, a public school for girls nearby that was socially a few octaves above Cranbrook, that one of his boys played the violin. Would it be a good idea for him to join Benenden's school orchestra? His Benenden colleague was amused and said "why not?" So in due course this was arranged. It was a matter of riding there by bicycle — less than an hour's ride — for rehearsals and for the end-of-term concert.

Words can hardly describe Otto's excitement when he bicycled there for the first time, wearing a straw hat, of course. They were rehearsing the Capriol Suite, by Peter Warlock, a beautiful contemporary serenade for strings. When the conductor introduced him he was overcome by shyness and remained shy with the girls until the end, and they with him. But he was extremely annoyed when in the next term the geography teacher Mr. Holtom, tall, blond and dashing, suddenly remembered that he played the clarinet and broke Otto's monopoly. He was not shy at all.

Otto's shyness was not the result of ignorance. He did know what a girl was, even though he was too old when he came to Cranbrook to attend the sex education lecture that Pop gave to the twelve-year-old new boys who entered Cornwallis House. He always took them in small groups to the nearby Angley Park. His wife prepared picnic boxes for the occasion. As a progressive educator, he thought it important for the boys' future sex lives to learn the Facts of Life in pleasantly natural surroundings that discouraged, though they did not eliminate, snickering disbelief. He obtained the necessary diagrams from the books by Marie Stopes, the pioneer in birth control.

Otto had missed this event but he knew the Facts of Life anyway. However, this did not by any means diminish his shyness in the orchestra. No doubt it would have been no different had he attended one of Pop's picnics in Angley Park.

Pop and his causes remained a strong influence on him all his life.

It was entirely in character that, when Ida Netter was desperate to obtain a visa for the United Kingdom late in 1938, Pop wrote a letter to the Home Office to declare that he was prepared to employ her as a domestic servant.

+++

On his honeymoon in 1948 Otto introduced his new wife, Sonia, to Pop and Mrs. Osborne in Oxford, where they lived in retirement.

15

Wittgenstein's Neighbour

From a radio interview broadcast in Cambridge in October 1957 on the weekly program "The University before the War":

Interviewer
Mr. Koch, is this the first time you're back in Cambridge?

Koch
No, I have been back two or three times since the war. But this visit has special significance for me. I went there exactly twenty years ago. I was just eighteen.

Interviewer
And you spent the full three undergraduate years here?

Koch (hesitating)
Well, yes.

Interviewer
I mean, did you graduate in 1940?

Koch
Yes, I did.

Interviewer
Good. In this series we are interviewing many of your contemporaries, and also older alumni, in order to get a sense of the university before the war. But you are my first guest who came to Cambridge from Germany.

Koch
Not directly. I had already spent two years in an English public school.

Interviewer (looks at his notes)
Oh you did? I didn't know that.

Koch

If you want to interview a German who was sympathetic to Nazi Germany and came to Cambridge, I'm afraid I'm not your man. I was a Jewish refugee.

Interviewer (confused)

Oh, I see. Did you know pro-Nazi Germans in Cambridge?

Koch

As a matter of fact, I did not. There must have been some.

Interviewer

Oh, I'm sure. Not only Germans. What was your college?

Koch

St. John's.

Interviewer

Why did you pick St. John's?

Koch

It was my headmaster's old college.

Interviewer

And what did you read?

Koch

In my first year I studied economics and then I switched to law.

Interviewer

Do you think those were wise choices?

Koch

In retrospect, no. I would never have chosen economics if my family had not thought it would help me in my future life as a businessman. I soon found out it would do nothing of the kind. First-year economic theory seemed to me either self-evident or unintelligible. That is why I started studying law, which I found more to my taste. But I did not think I would ever be a lawyer. In those years it was impossible to think straight about the future, anyway. It looked very bleak indeed. For that matter, it was also very difficult to think straight about the present.

Interviewer

That is exactly what interests me. What went on in your mind as the storm was gathering? Did you know there was going to be a war?

Koch

My life was entirely overshadowed by what was going on in Germany. I tried not to talk about it too much. And other people didn't talk to me about it either, out of some sort of consideration. But even I hoped against hope, against all reasonable expectations, that by some miracle we would be spared another war. It was the Spanish civil war that agitated us. That was in the daily news. Not some future war. Those were the years when half the student population said they would not fight for "King and Country" if called up to do so.

Interviewer

How did you feel about that?

Koch

I couldn't understand it. Still, my sympathies were with the Left. The Left was more anti-fascist than the Right. And I was still under the influence of one of my teachers whom I liked very much. He was a passionate socialist. But I was too much of an outsider to take part in student politics. When I talk of those days now at parties, I always get a laugh when I say that I was so much of an outsider that no Soviet agent ever solicited me to spy for them.

Interviewer (laughs)

You were a bit late for that. That happened a year or two before your time.

Koch

I know. Let me tell you a story. For Christmas 1938, one of my friends, John Gorringe, invited me to his home in Amersham, in Buckinghamshire. That was the first and only time that I could observe close up family life among the English gentry. I was hugely impressed, especially by the open way in which they welcomed me, a total stranger. I was really touched. But they could never quite understand who I was. I had a German accent — so I had to be German, no? They asked me one evening at dinner whether I wasn't proud of what my country had achieved in recent years. I said no, not exactly. (This was a month or so after Crystal Night, when they burned all the synagogues and arrested thousands.) And when I said that unless there was a miracle there was going to be another war, Mr. Gorringe — who had been in the First World War — threw his napkin on the table and said, "So you want John to get killed in another war?" and left the room.

Interviewer
Oh, how terrible! That must have been awful for you.

Koch
Yes, it was. I was so upset my friend's mother put her hand over mine.

Interviewer
So what do you now feel when you think of your three years at Cambridge?

Koch
I feel sad that circumstances made it impossible for me to get the most out of them. I mean, there I was, in one of the most beautiful places in the world, among the brightest of the bright, fully aware that I was incredibly fortunate, quite undeservedly so, yet unable to enjoy it properly. It was wasted on me. I blame myself for missing a golden opportunity. Also, I chose the wrong subjects to study. I mean, wrong for me. I should have studied comparative literature, or history, or philosophy. Wittgenstein was right next door, at Trinity. And I never heard of him.

Interviewer
You had that in common with most of your contemporaries.

Koch
Yes, but I had heard of Keynes and I never met him either. He had nothing to do with undergraduates. I did play the second violin in a performance of *Figaro* in the Art Theatre, which Keynes had founded.

Interviewer (amused)
So there was some connection. Were there any girls in the orchestra?

Koch
I am sure there were.

Interviewer
I only ask because before the war women could not be members of the university. And there were only two colleges to which girls could go. Only girls. Now, you don't have to answer this question. But did you have any girlfriends when you were at Cambridge?

Koch
I don't mind answering at all. In my first year I was totally enthralled by an enchanting girl from Berlin. But I did not know how to tell her how I felt about her. We always sat together in class. And when she missed a lecture I gave her my notes to copy. We were not Victorians but relations between boys and girls were not as uninhibited as they are nowadays. So I can't really call her a girlfriend, in today's sense of the word.

Interviewer
You mean, you had a crush on her. That also happens today.

Koch
I know. But "crush" is really the wrong word. I was deeply serious about her. She had a similar background to mine. And she was very ambitious. I was sure she was more interested in English boys than in someone like me. She had also gone to an English school and hardly had a German accent any more. After our first year we rarely saw each other again. She switched to psychology.

Interviewer
And apart from her, did you have any other women friends?

Koch
I did. But I was not serious about any of them.

Interviewer
Thank you, Mr. Koch. You gave me an excellent idea of what your life as an undergraduate was like, in Cambridge before the war. I am very grateful.

+++

In due course, Hilde Littauer, the lady in question, married an eminent virologist, originally from Berlin, and became Professor of Social Psychology at the London School of Economics. In 1957 she made her reputation, as Hilde Himmelweit, as the author of *Television and the Child,* the first scholarly work on the subject in England or North America.

In the early 'eighties, when I was in London, I phoned her. I gave her my name.

"Who?"

I repeated my name.

"I'm terribly sorry," she said, "but I'm afraid I don't remember you."

I mentioned the names of a few common friends.

A little light was switched on in her memory.

"Why don't you come to tea on Sunday afternoon," she suggested. "Around four."

I said I was delighted.

She gave me the address, Abingdon Road in Kensington, and asked whether I drank Chinese or Ceylon tea. I said Ceylon.

I was there at four.

The door opened. Her daughter opened it. My heart stopped. It was Hilde at eighteen!

Once again, I was tongue-tied. The girl excused herself and rushed off.

Hilde did remember me, after all. Vaguely. We had a polite, perfunctory conversation.

I had a much better time with her husband.

16

Tchaikovsky's Fifth

While I was at school in Cranbrook and at university in Cambridge I spent all my holidays in Frankfurt — until Easter 1938 — although it remained my home town only in a tenuous sense. In 1934 my sister, Margo, by then twenty-two, had gone to Paris, where she fell in love with Paul, a refugee from Cologne who had just finished his law studies when Hitler came to power. She married him in May 1936. They left France to return to Germany, not to Frankfurt but to Cologne, in preparation for their emigration to the United States, via England.

My brother left for the United States in 1937.

My mother was in Frankfurt and so was her mother, my grandmother Anna Kahn, who was looking after her ten-year-old grandson Wolf, the youngest child of Emil, who was struggling to build up a new career as a musician in New York. His second wife, Ellen Beck, and Wolf's three siblings in Stuttgart were to join Emil later.

Jews were gradually being deprived of their rights and humiliated in a thousand ways. The Nuremberg Laws of 1935 for the "Protection of the Race," for example, forbade Jewish families to have "Aryan" maids under the age of forty-five lest the race be polluted by their male employers. Everybody knew somebody who was in a concentration camp. People asked themselves whether the world would permit this nightmare to last. Most were actively planning their emigration, hoping to find a country that would grant them a visa. Many countries said no. Others imposed impossible conditions. The United States demanded affidavits. The search for distant, long-forgotten American relatives was a constant subject of conversation. In 1936, Jewish children, no longer allowed in the public schools, had to switch to Jewish schools. Whenever possible, Jews sent their children abroad.

In 1937, I spent part of my summer holidays in the Koch jewelry store. A swastika flag was waving on a building opposite. I was supposed to absorb the rudiments of a business in which it was hoped, without any real conviction and mainly to keep up our morale, that I would somehow be able to be engaged somewhere outside Germany, on Bond Street in London perhaps — my Cranbrook and Cambridge friends would no doubt form the nucleus of a rewarding clientèle — or on Fifth Avenue in New York.

In the surrealistic game I was playing — no, this was not a dream, it really happened — I sat in a corner of the store without anybody talking to me and learned only one thing: always make sure somebody else is in the store when facing a customer, in case of trouble. Of course, I was not equipped to serve any customers myself. In spite of the national boycott on April 1, 1933, when stormtroopers were planted outside Jewish stores all over Germany to intimidate people from buying from Jews, I was surprised how many customers remained loyal. The Koch name still had magic.

+++

Beginning in the early spring of 1933, Jewish artists, writers, musicians and actors and all others engaged in cultural activities were gradually dismissed from public institutions and instructed to serve only Jewish audiences and deal only with Jewish subject matter. They were to operate under the guidance of the Ministry of Propaganda and Enlightenment headed by Dr. Goebbels. A *Reichskulturverwalter* [culture guardian] was appointed, charged with the responsibility of purging the arts and media of Jews and to push the Jews into new ghettos. The man chosen was Hans Hinkel, an S.S. *Sturmbannführer* who had participated in Hitler's Beer Hall *Putsch* in Munich in November 1923. Already in June 1933 he was said to be so influential that one Nazi activist called him *de facto* minister of culture for Prussia. Hinkel considered "the Jew to be the eternal parasite and homeless master of lies," but at the same time he admired the vitality of the German Jewish community and respected individual members. During the war Hinkel married a woman who, for some reason, had been in a concentration camp.

It is possible that she was "non-Aryan." Goebbels never trusted him completely.

The Jewish organizations that emerged were the *Kulturbunde.* Increasingly they assumed enormous importance in the shrinking Jewish world. Hinkel's work was not easy. The line between Jewish and non-Jewish audiences was relatively easy to draw, but to differentiate German art from Jewish art was considerably more difficult. Hinkel and the Jewish leaders were rarely on the same wavelength. But their meetings were reasonably civil, certainly at first. To discharge his responsibilities Hinkel had to rely on factors other than common knowledge and commonsense. They agreed that Mendelssohn was incontrovertibly of Jewish descent and was therefore allowed, never mind that he wrote the Reformation Symphony and that his style was entirely "German." On the other hand, Hinkel had a problem with Handel. In his oratorios *Solomon, Esther, Deborah* and *Saul* and others he allowed himself to deal with Old Testament subjects. Would Hinkel allow the *Kulturbund* to play Handel, presumably a pure "Aryan" even if misguided? At first he was lenient, but by the spring of 1937 Bach, Beethoven and Brahms were no longer allowed. By the end of the year Schumann was also *verboten,* followed by Mozart and Schubert in the spring of 1938.

In theatre, a natural choice was the eighteenth-century Enlightenment classic *Nathan der Weise* by Gotthold Ephraim Lessing, a friend of Moses Mendelssohn. It preached tolerance and equated the values of the three great monotheistic religions, Christian, Jewish and Islamic. Hinkel never questioned its legitimacy for the *Kulturbund.* Many of them chose it as the first play in their theatrical programs. However, the increasingly influential Zionist voices among critics in the Jewish press — no reviewing of *Kulturbund* presentations was allowed in the non-Jewish press — had serious criticisms of such programming. And so did many in the audience. Was it not essential for Jews to create new works, in response to new challenges, instead of digging up old potboilers that created illusions and celebrated assimilation, a policy that was being exploded before our very eyes? Should we not be grateful to Hinkel for teaching Jews that priceless lesson, long overdue?

+++

Art, the Sister of Religion — that was the dogma of assimilated Frankfurt Jews, we Kochs among them, who identified their Jewishness primarily in cultural rather than in religious terms. Our consciences did not object to synagogues being used for concerts, plays and art exhibitions.

Our synagogue was the Westend Synagoge in the Freiherr von Steinstrasse, sometimes ironically called the Freiherr von Stein Synagoge, the Freiherr von Stein being remembered as one of the most progressive Prussian reformer after the Napoleonic wars, the period when we emerged from the ghettos. In that synagogue our parents got married and we, as children, occasionally observed the High Holidays.

One day during the Easter holidays in 1938, my mother and I went to a concert there. It was increasingly difficult to gather the necessary talent for full orchestras — there was especially a shortage of brass players, which made it hard to perform any symphony of Mahler later than the first. Some of the early *Kulturbund* celebrities, the conductor Hans Wilhelm Steinberg for example, had been lured to the Palestine Symphony, which Toscanini and Huberman had founded, and so had some of the musicians. But it was remarkable that in Frankfurt, and elsewhere, despite the ever diminishing resources, the standard of performance remained admirably high.

On the day my mother and I went, Tchaikovsky's Fifth Symphony was on the program. Enough brass has been rounded up. During the first few bars of the second movement I suddenly bent over with a violent pain in my abdomen, as though I had been pierced by a needle. My mother, correctly assuming that I was suffering an appendicitis attack, led me out of the synagogue. She took a taxi home and phoned Dr. Victor Schmieden, our family surgeon, who was not Jewish but knew we were. He was the head of surgery at the university's medical school in which my uncle, Richard Koch, had been the first professor of the history of medicine. Dr. Schmieden demanded that she take me to his hospital immediately — the municipal hospital, not the Jewish hospital. I was admitted, no questions asked. (Jewish patients were no longer allowed in non-Jewish hospitals.) I was to be operated on first thing in the morning, to prevent perforation.

Just before the anesthetist put a mask on my face to make me inhale ether, Dr. Schmieden came in.

I was still awake.

The last sound I heard was his greeting to his staff:

"Heil Hitler."

I was told later, but cannot corroborate, that in the 'twenties Josef Mengele had been one of his interns.

17

1938 Annus Horribilis: Part One

From a letter to my brother, Robert, in New Orleans, written in Lausanne, Switzerland, on August 10th, 1938.

...Yes, in Zürich I had to share a sordid *chambre garni* with M [Mutti, i.e., Mother]. Unprecedented. It was equipped with a primitive kitchen and was situated not exactly in the slums but close to them. A little different from our previous visits to Switzerland! But we did not mind *that* at all. The terrible thing was M's anguish — should she go back to Frankfurt, or stay here, safe but penniless, knowing that sooner or later the Swiss would send her back to Germany anyway, unless she could be admitted to another country. And how could *that* be arranged — from *here*??

I need not spell out the obvious. How could she leave Grandmother behind in Frankfurt, and Uncle L [the lawyer Ludwig Heilbrunn, our mother's brother-in-law, who had recently lost his wife and to whom she was close]?

And then there was a vitally important practical problem — the smuggling out from Frankfurt to Amsterdam of the watch collection, piece by piece, by Hans Heidt, a loyal and quick-witted anti-Nazi "Aryan" employee of Robert Koch, who had friends in the Party and was prepared to take risks for M. He had already got some of them out. She could only organize the rest of the shipments once she was back in Frankfurt. This could not be done from Zürich.

Would it not be better to emigrate legally — even if it meant having only ten marks in her purse? After all, some of her assets were abroad. At least, if she went back, she could have all her things properly packed in boxes and sent to England.

But Zürich was full of stories about Jews being arrested at all hours, especially at the border. These could not all be invented. Would she provoke Fate by going back? Thousands would have given *anything* to be where she was now — free!

Her indecision was agonizing. She was in an awful state, simply awful. And she looked terrible. If only we had had separate rooms! I would not have had to listen to the groans in her sleep, and to her mumblings that — can you believe it? — sounded very much like prayer! She had reverted to the almost catatonic condition she was in after Emil Netter's death two years ago, when for weeks she could not write letters to me in Cranbrook because she could not hold the pen. And when at last she could write, I could hardly decipher the handwriting!

You can imagine the talk among the refugees in the cafés, one horror story after another. But not all the talk was grim. I went to see a political cabaret, modelled on Erika Mann's *Pfeffermühle* — I think it's now in the States — which I thought tremendous. The satire of the Nazis certainly made me feel better. There was so much laughter! It was such a relief. And the music was terrific. It's certainly good to know that there are many in the same boat. Things are much worse when one is alone. À *propos* Erika Mann, I keep smiling about her father, Thomas Mann, landing in New York and telling reporters, without the usual irony, *I am the true Germany — not they.*

Yes, I saw Rudolf here in Lausanne, before he left for Amsterdam where Lore, who's gone ahead, has found a small apartment. I think by now the *Aryanization* [forced sale to an Aryan] of Robert Koch has been signed and sealed, but it won't do us any good because not a *pfennig* of the proceeds — a fraction of the real value, anyway — can be taken out of Germany. It's all in

Sperrmark [blocked marks]. Rudolf himself conducted the negotiations, with a reputable purchaser ... I have scribbled down the name somewhere. He thinks we did as well as could be expected under the circumstances. Such an arrangement, he says, is better for us than to have the government seize it. I don't quite understand in what way. I've heard talk about people like us making semi-legal deals with the purchaser where some of the money is paid out in *Devisen* [hard currency], but I am in no position to criticize Rudolf. I am sure you agree. I have no doubt he did as well as he could. He has contacts in Amsterdam and hopes to be able to continue dealing in precious stones and pearls, and he also intends to go into the book-buying-and-selling business, for which he may very well be better qualified.

I was sorry not to see Lore. Rudolf said some of her relatives have intensified the pressure on her to divorce him. You can imagine the tone in which he talks about that: "I think the woman is crazy not to listen to her family's perfectly sensible advice. She has all kinds of cousins high up in the *Wehrmacht*. Some no doubt go hunting boar with Goering in the wild forests of East Prussia. Why should she go into exile with me and live in penury? I think she is out of her mind!"

Rudolf talked to me as though it was understood that Nature had designated me as the Heir Apparent. I have done nothing to disabuse him of that assumption but it's really rather absurd, considering...

After the spring term was over I went to Belgium, to Knokke-Le-Zoute, staying at a cheap pension near the beach, to await a phone call from a Monsieur Rappaport in Antwerp, a business acquaintance of Rudolf's, who had apparently agreed to take me on for the summer as an apprentice, to learn something about diamonds and pearls. I spent a week or so on the beach, bored to tears, ready to leave at any moment for Antwerp. There were some other refugees there who told me that they

had heard of non-Aryan young people like me being
arrested at the border if they tried to return to Germany.
Monsieur Rappaport did not call, but Rosenbaum did —
he had just been in Frankfurt and was calling from Paris.
[Peter Rosenbaum had been in my class in the Goethe
Gymnasium.] He said the Gestapo had visited M and had
asked where I was. As you may remember, I was still
officially domiciled in Frankfurt, not yet *abgemeldet* [i.e.,
I had not legally emigrated]. She told the Gestapo I was
studying abroad. That's too bad, the man said, because
I was being called up for military service — *Ersatzreserve
Zwei* [Ersatz Reserve No. 2] — and if I didn't appear within
two weeks — I *think* he said two weeks — certain steps
would have to be taken. I asked Rosenbaum whether
this was to be interpreted as a threat against M. He said
my guess was as good as his. Of course, there had been a
slight mistake in the military bureaucracy because Jews
are not eligible to serve even in the *Ersatzreserve Zwei*.
But this could only be cleared up by a personal visit. So,
without further ado, and without first phoning M, I took
the train to Frankfurt. If she had known this she would
have become sick with worry. I must admit I, too, was a
trifle nervous at the border. But nothing happened. At the
station in Cologne I was sorely tempted to get out of the
train during the fifteen-minute stop and phone Margo and
Paul, who were still there, waiting for their American visa,
but I didn't want to draw any stormtrooper's attention to
my presence by getting in and out of the train.

You cannot imagine how delighted M was to see
me. She immediately decided that the day after
my appearance at the *Polizeipräsidium* to legitimate
my change of domicile, she would take the train to
Switzerland and Italy with me for a short holiday. She
immediately went to the bank to procure the necessary
Kreditbriefe [hard currrency].

So the next morning I went to the *Polizeipräsidium*, on
the Platz der Republik, opposite the Goethe Gymnasium.

I cannot deny that my stomach was full of butterflies.
I had never before been inside the building. Endless
corridors, populated by innumerable policemen. At last
I found the office. An elderly officer greeted me politely.
A secretary retrieved my file in no time. On the cover of
it was a big J. My butterflies multiplied.

The officer asked me, in pleasant Frankfurt dialect,
where abroad I was being educated. I told him. He
nodded. "So you want to change your domicile." I said
yes, I did. He nodded again and stamped the document in
front of him. How long was I going to stay in Frankfurt?
I said I was leaving for Switzerland the next day.

"My, you are lucky." He rose from his chair to shake
hands with me. [In Frankfurt slang he said *"Sie habbe
Schwein,"* you have pig. I suppose for some reason pigs
stand for luck in many languages. Hence piggybanks.]

"Have a good trip. And good luck!"

No need to describe my feelings.

So the next morning, we went to Switzerland and then
to Florence. And you know the rest — what happened
after we returned to Zürich and ran out of money and had
to borrow while residing in the above-mentioned sordid
chambre garni.

In Florence, we went to see Kurt Stern (a music-loving
friend of our mother's, a lawyer from Karlruhe, who had
married the daughter of a Jewish-Italian manufacturer
with a factory in Prato, an industrial town near Florence).
He had written to her several times, complaining of
desperate homesickness for Karlsruhe. He did not seem
to be worried as yet about Mussolini's recently acquired
anti-Semitism.

I have tried to tell the following story to several people
who don't see the point even though I explain in detail,
and with great emphasis, that in Germany operas are
invariably presented in German, whatever the original
language.

This is the story.

We were the guests of a friend who had hit the jackpot but was suffering from lethal homesickness for Karlsruhe. He was married to a rich lady by the name of Gemma who loved him. We were sitting on the balcony of his apartment, half way up the hill to Fiesole, with a view below us of one of the most beautiful cities in the world. The sun was setting.

The door to the living room was open. The radio was on. We heard the strains of an opera — direct from La Scala in Milan.

"Can you imagine," our friend exclaimed in a melodramatically tearful voice drenched in self-pity, "Rigoletto *in Italian!*"...

+++

A few weeks later Kurt and Gemma Stern left for England. To please Hitler, Mussolini had brought in anti-Semitic legislation.

At the beginning of the war Gemma went ahead to New York. A few months later Kurt at last found space on a boat and embarked to follow her. The boat was torpedoed. He was saved. Two months later he tried again. The second boat was also torpedoed.

This time he was not saved.

Otto Koch
1914

Otto Koch

Ida Koch (née Kahn)
1914

The Brothers Koch
Robert and Otto (Eric)

Mother and the three Koch children:
Margo, Otto (Eric), Ida, Robert

Emil and Ida Netter

Nelly Kahn

Otto H. Kahn

Cranbrook School: "Pop" and boys

Wolf Kahn

Rudolf Heilbrunn

Louis Koch

Dr. Richard Koch

Ludwig Koch

A romance across the barbed wire fence started in Quebec City between Peter Field and Pauline Perrault. They exchanged love letters and Pauline often enclosed photographs of herself, some of them bearing messages such as the one above.

Peter then was transferred to Sherbrooke and in October 1941 was granted permission to leave the camp and spend the weekend with Pauline and her family in Quebec City.

Peter Field & Pauline Perrault
Quebec, October 1941

18

1938 Annus Horribilis: Part Two

On Friday September 23rd, my mother returned to Frankfurt from Zürich and I to England. The academic year did not begin until early October. Our family friends Max and Johanna Morel invited me to stay with them for a weekend in Weybridge, Surrey, half an hour south of London. Their son, Werner, was a schoolmate of Robert's and mine. Max was a banker who had left Frankfurt in good time, transferred his business to the City of London and had a nice house. He had been close to my stepfather, Emil Netter, and, somewhat presumptuously I thought, considered himself *in loco parentis*.

Morel
So you say you allowed your mother to go back to Frankfurt after Chamberlain and Hitler had a *tête-à-tête* in Bad Godesberg and swore eternal brotherhood.

Koch
That had nothing to do with it. She had agonized whether or not to return and, at last, made up her mind.

Morel
And you allowed it.

Koch
She is a grown person. And she is my mother!

Morel
Listen, Otto. You've just had your nineteenth birthday. You're no longer your mother's little boy. You're grown up now and you have to learn how to take responsibility. It was irresponsible of you to allow her to go back.

Koch
My mother has led her own life since my father's death. She is an independent woman. She was undecided for a long time and at last made up her mind.

Morel
And you say that meeting in Godesberg had nothing to do with it?

Koch
She had bought her ticket beforehand.

Morel
Once there is a war, Germany will close all its borders. Your mother will be trapped. And you will be responsible because you didn't stop her. There is nothing you can say that will change my mind about that! You can't be so naive as to believe that Chamberlain giving in to Hitler will lead to anything other than war. That is now inevitable.

+++

I had a severe gastric disturbance when I left the Morel house. It continued right through the Munich Agreement at the end of the month.

Editorial in the *Times,* October 1st, 1938

A New Dawn
No conquering hero from a victory on a battlefield
has come home adorned with nobler laurels than
Mr. Chamberlain from Munich yesterday, and King and
people alike have shown him by the manner of their
reception their sense of his achievement. The terms of
settlement of the Czech-German dispute reached in the
small hours of the morning ... had been seen to deliver
the world from a menace of extreme horror while doing
rough-and-ready justice between the conflicting claims.
Yet even this great service to humanity was already
beginning to appear as the lesser half of the Prime
Minister's work in Munich. He himself announced it as a
prelude to a larger settlement...

+++

Several days later, back in Cambridge, while I was getting ready for my second year, I had tea with my friend George L. Mosse, the grandson of the founder of the *Berliner Tageblatt*, which, before the Nazis, was one of Europe's great newspapers. I had not yet recovered from the gastric disturbance caused by Max Morel.

George was studying Tudor history. He did not live in college but in a cheap room in a sidestreet near the station, in a rooming house governed by his landlady, Mrs. Thompson. Like many well-endowed people, he hated to part with money.

George had invited me the previous spring to spend a few days with his father and stepmother in Paris. We had seen a lot of each other in my first year and I was not surprised to learn that he took a line very different from Max Morel.

Mosse
The first thing we historians learn is that you never know what's going to happen. You will never hear one of us use the word "inevitable," a word you say used by your friend the banker. There is always an infinite number of ways any situation can develop. As bankers should know.

Koch
So you think the *Times* is right?

Mosse
No, of course not. It's wishful thinking that any settlement with Hitler can work. He is incapable of keeping any treaty. As many people in Chamberlain's own party understand perfectly well. It's not only that they don't approve of any settlement based on the betrayal of our friends. But that doesn't mean that war is inevitable.

Koch
How can it be avoided? Hitler will make one demand after another. Sooner or later somebody has to say no. Then there will be a war.

Mosse
Yes, that is one possibility. But there are many others. The vast majority of the British public was hugely relieved when

99

Chamberlain came back with his piece of paper, not because people are stupid or cowardly or immoral, but because they feel, quite rightly, that the country is not ready for war and that Chamberlain gained us time. The *Times* went too far, of course, but in a sense that is what it is also saying. When I say "us," I mean the world, the entire world. Time to arm, for one thing. But also time to think things through. Time to think of alternatives to war.

Koch
What do you mean?

Mosse
What about the British and the French making a real effort to get in touch with Hitler's opponents in the army and have him gently, or not so gently, disposed of? If Gandhi can make life uncomfortable for the British in India, maybe we can help the German resistance use similar methods. You can't tell me that there aren't very considerable moral forces that can be mobilized against Hitler. There have already been some attempts to bump him off.

Koch
Suppose a Jew tried it and failed...

Mosse
I shudder to think.

At that moment my gastric disturbance flared up once again. I had to excuse myself to go to the bathroom. While I was there for a little while I heard a curious noise outside the door. I paid no attention. But then there was a knock.

"Sir," Mrs. Thompson said, "do you have to use all my lavatory paper?"

I still cannot think of the Munich Agreement without thinking of that.

+++

About a month later the seventeen-year-old Herschel Grynspan shot Third Secretary Ernst vom Rath in the German embassy in Paris. The diplomat died two days later. Grynspan had intended to kill the German ambassador. But he was not in his office. So he shot vom Rath instead. Grynspan's parents had been among the seventeen thousand Jews of Polish citizenship, many of whom had lived in Germany for decades, who had been arrested, had their property seized and were sent to the Polish border. The Poles refused to accept them.

Goebbels used this assassination to unleash the *Kristallnacht,* the night of the broken glass, when all over Germany synagogues were burned and thousands of Jews were arrested and sent to concentration camps.

As I found out later, my sister, Margo, and her husband, Paul, in Cologne, managed to escape before the police arrived. They jumped into their car when they heard about approaching trouble and drove along back roads to Frankfurt to stay with my mother. All three remained unmolested.

The Frankfurt opera singer Hans Erl was not so lucky. I remembered him well. He was a huge man who sang Ochs in the *Rosenkavalier* and Sarastro in *The Magic Flute.* He had lost his job in 1933.

In the early morning of November 10th, he was among those who had been brought by truck to the *Festhalle,* the Exhibition Grounds, where by then hundreds of men had been made to scrub the floor and were being humiliated in other ways before being taken to the camps. On arrival, Erl was "interviewed" by an S.S. man.

"What's your name?"

"Hans Erl."

"What's your profession?"

"I sang bass in the Opera."

"Oh really?" The S.S. man mulled this over. At last he said: "Well then, sing something!"

Erl drew himself to his full height and began:

In diesen heil'gen Hallen
Kennt man die Rache nicht.
Und ist ein Mensch gefallen
Führt Liebe ihn zur Pflicht.
Dann wandelt er an Freundes Hand
Vergnügt und froh ins bess're Land.

[In these hallowed halls
One does not know revenge
And should a man have fallen
Love will guide him to duty.
Then he wanders holding the hand of a friend
Cheerfully and happily into a better land.]

Everyone in the hall — victims and executioners — stopped in their tracks, galvanized.

"You sang well," the S.S. man whispered to Erl. "Run!"

Erl followed the suggestion.

+++

On June 10th, 1942, Hans Erl and his wife, Sofia, were arrested and deported to Majdanek. The date of their death is unknown.

His bust is in the Frankfurt Opera House.

+++

In February, my mother arrived in London, with her brother-in-law Ludwig Heilbrunn, the lawyer. As it turned out, her decision in Zürich to take the risk and return home had been the right one. She was still able to help her mother apply for a visa to the United States, organize the dispatch of the remainder of the watch collection and have her things packed in boxes and sent off. She could not know that they would never reach their destination.

Around the same time, Margo and Paul arrived in London, en route to the United States. There was just enough money available to rent a small apartment for all of them in North End House, on the Fulham Road in West Kensington, between Hammersmith and Olympia.

Ludwig was nearly seventy and had a heart condition. His spoken English was serviceable but not good.

Opposite North End House was a funeral home. In the window it advertised its services by proclaiming "A well-conducted funeral need not be expensive."

Ludwig learned this phrase by heart and repeated it on every occasion to perfect his spoken English.

Every morning he read the Court Gazette in the *Times*. One day he noted that his namesake Ludwig Koch, the first cosin of his late wife and my father, was invited to a garden party at Buckingham Palace. Relations between our part of the family and Ludwig Koch had ruptured long ago. He was considered a black sheep because he was said to keep an alligator in his bathtub. An eccentric fondness for animals was certainly not customary in our circles. But in England, apparently, one could never love animals enough. That is why his frequent broadcasts on the BBC, in a thick Frankfurt accent, presenting his adventurous recordings of birdsong, had become immensely popular.

Ludwig Heilbrunn's house in Frankfurt was on the Niedenau.

"The King invites this lunatic to his garden party," he exclaimed, shaking his head in mock disbelief when he read about Ludwig Koch's invitation to Buckingham Palace. "The man was never allowed to cross my threshold in the Niedenau! What kind of a country have I come to?"

19

The Famous Koch

"So you're Otto's son." Ludwig Koch examined my face closely when I went to see him in his apartment. Everyone, simply everyone, had been asking me in the last two years whether I was related to Ludwig Koch, by far the most famous Koch so far. So it was about time. My mother and Ludwig Heilbrunn did not object.

I liked him immensely the moment I saw him. I knew his sister, Rosie, but I had never met him. There were certain family characteristics I recognized immediately. He had my grandfather's brown eyes, but the shape of his face was oval, not round.

"I was fond of your father, you know," he said. "We had the same violin teacher, Eduard Broeckl, and we occasionally played together. If he had lived, the family would not have split and we would all still be the best of friends."

I looked puzzled.

"You see, there were four Koch brothers and one sister when they came to Frankfurt from Geisa. Some decided what mattered most was to make money and rise in society. Others thought the pursuit of science and the arts was more important. Your grandfather, Robert, and his younger brother Louis went in for the money. Dorchen became a pianist and my father, Karl, a scientist, even though he had to make his living as a businessman. Not very successfully, I'm sorry to say. I became both a scientist and an artist. But for making money I never had any talent."

"And my father?"

"Otto would never have become a great jeweller," Ludwig replied. "His heart was in horse jumping and in his violin. And in being a chivalrous gentleman. Never in money, or society. I liked him a lot."

I said I was touched to hear it and added how delighted I was that, at last, he had created a role for himself that got him the recognition he had never achieved in pre-Nazi Germany. And that he no doubt deserved. But surely this was due to his being a natural scientist rather than an artist.

"But," he retorted, "I would never had got to my birds if I had not been an artist first."

I asked him to explain.

"I started life as a *Wunderkind*. I think the first and only *Wunderkind* in the Koch family. Unless you..."

"Oh no!" I laughed. "Far from it."

"That's just as well. *Wunderkinder* have tough lives. I must have been three or four when I was taken to see Franz Liszt, a year before he died. He had come to Frankfurt to assist in a performance of his oratorio *Christus*. He was tall man with white hair, and he was wearing his vestments. He kissed me. I have since read that when Liszt was eleven Czerny took him to Vienna to see Beethoven. There Liszt played for him and Beethoven kissed him."

"So indirectly," I could not help observing, "Beethoven kissed you. Via Liszt."

"Absolutely," he beamed. "You're a bright boy. You'll go far. I played the violin so well that the great Joseph Joachim gave me a dedication after hearing me play Spohr's eighth violin concerto. That was before I took singing lessons and before I became just as proficient as singer of *Lieder* and opera singer as I had been as a violinist. But I am getting ahead of myself. Music alone did not fill my life. When I was eight my father took me to the Leipzig Fair and bought me an Edison phonograph and a box of wax cylinders. I soon had the original idea of asking people to give me their autograph by sound, on a cylinder. That is how I managed to collect a number of famous voices, such as the voice of the physicist Hermann von Helmholtz. I even approached the great Bismarck, who first took it as a joke. But then he played along. I wish I still had the recording of his high-pitched falsetto, so incongruous in that huge man."

"Oh, that would be invaluable now."

"Of course. But the Nazis deliberately destroyed my entire collection. It included many famous men and women and nearly fifty species of birds and other animals. Nothing survives. By the way, Brahms mentioned to someone when he came to Frankfurt that Edison's agent had recorded his playing of one of his Hungarian dances. This wax recording was brought to me just a few weeks before I left Germany three years ago. It was rapidly disintegrating, packed in a wooden box, padded with cotton wool. I transferred it to a disc. But the quality was so terrible that little of the playing could be heard."

"So you were a violinist," I said, "a singer and a recording pioneer. Did you also record animal voices?"

"I most certainly did. I obtained the voice of the *quagga*, a species between a horse and a zebra that is now extinct. We lived only a quarter of an hour from the zoo and I spent a lot of time there. But, of course, I also had a zoo of my own, with monkeys, pigeons and dozens of exotic reptiles and amphibia. And birds. I had an Indian *shama*, for example, a kind of throstle. And many other rare creatures."

"Your mother," I noted quietly, "must have been delighted with the mess they made."

"She made me clean it up. But you are right. I must have been a dreadful problem to her. Some people, no doubt including members of your part of the family, refused to come and see us. Still, our place was always full of visitors. My mother never complained."

"With all this going on, how could you keep up your interest in music?"

"I never found that difficult. I tried to go to all the concerts. Frankfurt was an exceptionally musical city. One day I had an amazing experience. Tsar Nicholas came to Darmstadt. He was visiting his brother-in-law, the Grand Duke of Hesse. I knew the Grand Duke because he was a talented musician. He invited me. Few people remember today that the Tsar was a very good singer, with a nice Slavic timbre. The Grand Duke accompanied him on the piano. The Tsar was shy and did not like anybody to listen to him. But the Grand Duke allowed me to listen from another room. I'll never forget it."

"When you performed," I asked, "were you ever shy like the Tsar? Did you ever have stage fright?"

"Of course. Most artists do. I often discussed this with Caruso, and with many of the performers in Bayreuth, where I spent a lot of time. I greatly admired Cosima Wagner's productions of her husband's works and I also made friends with their son, Siegfried. Once, when I was walking with Cosima in the garden of the Villa Wahnfried, some swans flew overhead. Cosima said it was the sharp rhythm of the swans' wings that had inspired her husband to compose *The Ride of the Valkyries.*"

What a treasure this man was, I thought. How unfortunate that we never knew him when we were children.

"And you also sang in operas?"

"I certainly did. I was a great success as Mephisto in Gounod's *Faust.* I also sang in many oratoria. The critics wrote I was the best interpreter of the bass part in Haydn's *Creation* they had ever heard. And I performed in the first performance, in Augsburg, of Gabriel Pierné's *St. François d'Assise.* Once I sang in a sports arena to an audience of thousands, accompanied by an excellent orchestra under the composer Max Bruch. I chose an aria from *Don Carlo* and a few Schubert *Lieder.* My soft notes penetrated the entire hall. I never used force. I must confess I was rather pleased with myself."

"No doubt with good reason. And was it the music in birds' song that attracted you to them?"

"Oh no, not in the sense you mean. I learned early on that bird songs have nothing to do with our music. I once explained this to Fritz Kreisler. The Queen Mother of Belgium had brought us together. He wanted to write down the notation of a blackbird's song. I told him that was impossible. Birds have intervals that we cannot reproduce with any of our instruments. We can only approximate them. But the main point is that it's not the pitch that identifies a bird's song but its timbre. That can only be preserved in recordings, not in notation, and not by any musical instrument. Not so far, anyway."

I looked at my watch. "Oh, I'm sorry," I exclaimed. "I'm keeping you too long. And I haven't yet had a chance to ask you about your military and diplomatic career."

"That was just as eventful but much of it I can't talk about. Perhaps I should begin with the year 1909, when I took singing lessons from a teacher who lived in Bad Homburg. Once, after my lesson, when I visited my teacher's father, I found him sitting in front of a small house talking to another man. He happened to be none other than King Edward VII. He had just had a meeting with the Kaiser and Admiral Tirpitz. I heard him say, 'This morning's meeting means war.' A year later he died. So I knew before most other people what was going to happen."

"What is it that you can't talk about?"

"I managed to be trained as an intelligence officer. You see, I speak French without any trace of a foreign accent. So don't ask me what I did during the war. But I can talk about what I did the day after the Armistice was signed. I had become an expert on all matters concerning prisoners of war. So I was appointed Chief Delegate for Repatriation and Liaison Officer for the French-occupied zone. I had dealings with Clemenceau, with Poincaré, Foch, Joffre, Pétain and Maginot, and on one occasion with the American General Pershing. So you can see that in the years following 1918 I had to neglect my birds. But I did find time to assist in the rebuilding of international musical life. In 1925 I gave up my work for the government and accepted an appointment with the City Council of Frankfurt to organize exhibitions. And I resumed my recording activities. Until I left for England in 1936. But all this will have to wait for another occasion."

I rose from my chair.

"I'm sorry I kept you so long," I said.

"Oh not at all. Before you go, I must tell you one more thing. My semi-diplomatic career had brought me into close touch with Field Marshall Hindenburg, who as you know became President of Germany in 1925. He was a great huntsman. One day he asked me to record the roar of stags and deer. I did so, but he found the noise too harsh and asked me to try again. But I did not want to bother the old man with the result. He was eighty-four and I thought he must have the 'Bohemian corporal' — that is what he called Hitler — more on his mind than the sound of stags and deer. But no. His Secretary of State, Dr. Meissner, called me and said the Field Marshall wanted to hear my recording. So I went there. This time he was completely satisfied. He kept me for hours and told me stories from his life. Soon afterward he died."

20

Cambridge and (the) Wolf

Between *Kristallnacht* in November 1938 and the outbreak of war in September 1939, about ten thousand unaccompanied, mostly Jewish, children from Germany, Austria, Czechoslovakia and Poland were welcomed in England. Later this program was to become known as the *Kindertransport*. No other country was as generous.

In the spring of 1939 my eleven-year-old cousin, Wolf Kahn, was still in Frankfurt. After the defection of his mother, Nelly, within a year of his birth he had been brought up by our mutual grandmother. His father, stepmother and siblings were in New York. I was the logical person to look after him in England.

In May, I went to see Mrs. Deborah Bernstein, in the office of the Cambridge Refugee Committee, and filled out a form. She was one of the volunteer ladies who found families for the new arrivals. Wolf was expected to come at any time with the *Kindertransport*.

"How is his English?" Mrs. Bernstein asked me.

"Excellent." I explained that Wolf had learned the language from Ethel Wilkins, universally known as Mim, a contraction of "miss" and "mum," who was our grandmother's English companion and had been engaged as a governess for Wolf's father and my mother long before the Great War.

"Good," said Mrs. Bernstein. "That makes our work considerably easier. Will you be in Cambridge this summer to keep an eye on him?"

"I'm afraid not," I replied. "I will be in London during my vacation. But I'll be back to start my third year in October. We can keep in touch by phone. I can always come up any time."

"I don't think that will be necessary."

Mrs. Bernstein glanced at the form I filled out.

109

"I see he is going to a Jewish school in Frankfurt," she said.

"Yes. The *Philantropin*. Jewish children are no longer allowed to attend the ordinary schools."

"I know. Will it matter if we can't find a Jewish family for him?"

"Not at all," I replied. "He has not had a Jewish education."

She made a note.

"I don't suppose he will require special instruction on how to behave. We have a form here we give to all the refugees. Especially the grown-ups."

She passed it to me. I picked a paragraph at random. "Do not make yourself conspicuous by speaking loudly, nor by your manner or dress. The Englishman greatly dislikes ostentation, loudness of dress or manner ... He attaches very great importance to modesty, understatement in speech rather than overstatement ... He values good manners far more than he values evidence of wealth."

I smiled. "Mim will have conveyed all this to him," I said. "He is a delightful boy, very gifted, with a cheerful disposition."

"But surely he must be going through a lot," Mrs. Bernstein observed.

"Yes, he is. But every effort is being made to protect him and allow him to grow up as though conditions were reasonably normal. He knows, of course, that he isn't allowed in any public park or to go to the movies, or buy ice cream from the stand at the corner. None of this can be ignored. But his extraordinary ability to draw makes his life interesting, in spite of all these things. He is unusually talented, you know. He draws all the time. Naturally he finds Nazi uniforms and Nazi gala celebrations particularly rewarding subjects. However, a few ugly incidents could not be avoided. On at least one occasion some Nazi boys pushed him off his bicycle. He can easily be identified as a Jewish boy in the street, you know, not because he looks particularly Jewish — he doesn't — but because he does not wear the brown shirt of the Hitler Youth. After *Kristallnacht* his teachers were arrested and sent to the concentration camp in Buchenwald. They were released after four months in terrible shape, the hair shorn off, not allowed to say a word about the horrors they had seen and experienced. All this, no doubt, took its toll. Now, having to leave his grandmother and Mim behind will be awful. But when one is eleven and in good health, every new turn in life is an adventure. No doubt there will be a tearful scene at the station when they see him off, a little boy with his name tag on his chest. But it may be worse for the ladies who have to go back to the apartment and face the future without him."

I paused while Mrs. Bernstein looked at her list of names.

"We have a number of dons," she said, "who would like to welcome a refugee child. Professor Tomkins who teaches organic chemistry, for example. What's your field?"

Law, I said.

"Do you know Professor Wade?"

"I most certainly do," I cried. "He's my lecturer on constitutional law."

"He has put down his name."

"That would be very good!" I exclaimed. Wade was a pleasant, straightforward middle-aged academic with horn-rimmed glasses and pale blue eyes, who wore his hair parted in the middle. He was the author of the textbook we used. "Mind you, he doesn't know me," I continued, "I just attend his lectures, that's all. I'm not in his college. I'm at St. John's. He's at Gonville and Caius."

"I will talk to him," said Mrs. Bernstein. "I see he lives in Sawston, a little out of town, about six miles south of here. It'll certainly help if I say you're one of his students. Let's see what happens."

+++

Professor Wade agreed. Wolf arrived in June, one of many children with name tags on their chests. My mother was at Waterloo Station in London. The officials from the Refugee Committee allowed him to spend one night with her, in the apartment in North End House, and made her promise to deliver him again the next day to King's Cross Station so that they could escort him to Cambridge. There Mrs. Wade welcomed him. All this worked perfectly.

Throughout the summer Wolf was at Sawston Manor, a grand place, fully equipped with a tennis court in the large garden. I kept in touch with Mrs. Bernstein, to make sure that Wolf was alright. She said he was. Once or twice I spoke to him directly. He said he was fine, but there was something in his tone that was not altogether convincing. She discouraged me from phoning him too often, which seemed reasonable to me. I confess I was a bit concerned, but the overriding consideration was that Wolf was safe in England while the news from the Continent was getting worse and worse, after Hitler had broken the Munich Agreement in March, marched into Prague, and made Bohemia and Moravia German "protectorates." That made war overwhelmingly likely. In mid summer there were growing rumblings about Danzig.

I heard a number of stories about the *Kindertransport* — children having a difficult time. I was certain that, whatever the imperfections, if any, of Wolf's sojourn at Sawston Manor, he was better off than a boy of fourteen from Bremen who, I was told, was being used by his benefactor in Liverpool to spy on his wife and sent to bed without his supper if he did not provide the required information. And Wolf's fate, even if not idyllic, could hardly be as unfortunate as that of a girl of thirteen from Hanover, placed with a family in Tunbridge Wells, who was forced to act as full-time nurse to a bad-tempered old grandmother suffering from advanced dementia. Usually the ladies from the Refugee Committee intervened whenever they heard of such abuses, but very often they were not told about them until the situation had become intolerable.

When I arrived back in Cambridge in early October, after war had broken out in September, Mrs. Bernstein told me Wolf was no longer with the Wade family. She had found a new home for him. She apologized for not telling me about this before but she thought there was no need since she knew I would be back in time for my third year. The initiative had come from Professor Wade himself, who merely said he did not think the arrangement had worked very well. He did not give any reasons. Wolf's new family was in Histon, three miles north west of Cambridge, home of the Chivers jam factory. His new patron was William Purvis, a teacher of mathematics. Wolf had already been there for three weeks and been admitted to the Cambridge and County High School for Boys. He was to be number one in English in no time.

When I saw Wolf, just before his twelfth birthday, he was full of enthusiasm for the new family. Bill and Sybil Purvis insisted he call them Daddy and Mummy. He already felt completely at home with them and enjoyed the experience of going to an English school and learning how to play rugger. But he found the rules a bit confusing and wasn't sure whether he would ever be able to master them. As a matter of fact, in his first school report it was stated that he was "a keen forward who played not always according to the rules."

When I asked him what happened at the Wades, he said he would tell me in due course.

Wolf stayed with the Purvis family until April 1940, when he left for New York. Throughout the winter I saw him once or twice a month and enjoyed showing him Cambridge. He usually had his sketchbook with him and made drawings of the old college buildings, especially the picturesque, medieval gates. The sketches were astoundingly good. We talked a lot about the things we found strange in England — the obvious absurdity of driving on the wrong side of the road, the row houses and the slums in London that you could see from the train, the constant drinking of tea and the unappealing puddings we were expected to eat.

It was during these walks that I found out the details about his summer at Sawston Manor. Professor Wade had apparently expected a miserable, downtrodden, half-starved orphan and was not pleased when a cheerful, well-behaved, smiling, well-fed boy with a steamer-trunk full of clothes appeared, a boy, moreover, far better educated than his daughters. He felt he had been deceived. So he decided Wolf was to be a servant, to get up at five every morning to polish the shoes, to be a companion to the children and to help in the garden. Mrs. Wade followed her husband's lead, and so did three of the five daughters who considered him a nuisance and ordered him around. The fourth was Patience, who was five and liked him. The fifth was a baby. On one occasion, the baby fell off the swing while under Wolf's care. Professor Wade made him write a hundred times "In England a boy who leave little girls in distress is called a coward."

Wolf was constantly criticized for doing everything wrong. So it was only natural that he was acutely unhappy. Fortunately,

Professor Wade put an end to his misery soon after war had broken out. By then he had become an officer in the Home Guards. He asked Mrs. Bernstein to move the boy to another family.

When Mrs. Bernstein told me about all this she said she could not grasp how Professor Wade could have misunderstood her so completely. After all, he was supposed to have a clear legal mind. She had described Wolf's background to him beforehand, she said, in some detail. Apparently he wasn't listening.

When I saw Wolf off at the station when he was on his way to the United States I asked him what his most vivid memory will be of his summer in Sawston Manor.

He laughed.

"The time those awful girls put a frog in my bed."

+++

Today Wolf Kahn is a prominent painter in the United States. His lyrical and beautiful landscapes are among America's best-loved contemporary paintings. He is the author of *Wolf Kahn's America,* with a preface by John Updike.

For more than sixty years he has kept in touch with the Purvis family. Throughout the difficult postwar years in the UK he regularly sent them care parcels and, in recent years, has seen to it that Mrs. Purvis, since her husband's death, has a financially secure and comfortable old age.

21

False Alarm

Dramatis Personae:
Brian and Catherine Roland, grandparents
Retired Colonel Reginald Thornton
Dorothy King, a secretary
Kenneth Lorimer, a student pacifist
Otto Koch, a refugee
Ida Netter, a refugee and Otto Koch's mother
Ludwig Heilbrunn, a refugee lawyer and Ida Netter's brother-in-law

Every character carries a gas mask.

Scene: The basement of North End House, West Kensington, London. A few tenants of the apartment house have already assembled. Our characters sit at a table in the centre.

Time: Noon, Sunday, September 3rd, 1939. One hour earlier, Neville Chamberlain announced that England was now at war with Germany.

We hear the wailing of the air-raid siren.

Mrs. Roland
Oh dear, I think I left my handbag behind. Would you mind terribly going upstairs again and fetch it for me? I don't think I locked the apartment.

Mr. Roland
Don't be silly, Catherine. Nobody's going to steal it during an air raid.

Mrs. Roland
It's not that, dear. I need my pills.

Mr. Roland (offering her a cigarette)
That'll keep you calm.

The colonel arrives.

Colonel
I don't think we've met. Colonel Reginald Thornton.

The Rolands introduce themselves.

Colonel
Did you hear the prime minister? (They nod.) At last he's showing some backbone. Of course, this time he didn't have much choice. But I must say I was quite moved when he said that everything he's worked for, everything he's hoped for, has crashed into ruins. That's all too true. I understand the Poles have asked us to bomb every military installation in Germany. Right now. I hope we'll do it. You were in the last war, Mr. Roland?

Mr. Roland
From beginning to end.

Mrs. Roland
Who would have thought — only twenty-five years after 1914 — we'd have another war. (Shakes her head.) I'll never understand it. My heart nearly broke when we had to say goodbye to our grandchildren. They were evacuated on Thursday, to somewhere near Newcastle. How long do you think it's going to last, colonel?

Colonel
I won't make any predictions any more. I would never have believed Hitler and Stalin would gang up on us. Who could have foreseen that? I'd wager the people in the Foreign Office were just as surprised as I was. All I know is that we're going to win. I won't say any more.

Dorothy King arrives, wrapped in a towel.

Dorothy
Is this it?

Mrs. Roland
Who knows? Come and join us, dear. Make yourself at home. You might as well. We'll probably spend a lot of time together.

Dorothy

I was in my bath when I heard the sirens. (Looks around.) So we've all read the instructions in the lift.

Mr. Roland

Yes, we have. I don't suppose you had the radio on when you were in your bath and didn't hear the prime minister. We're at war with Germany. And have been for one hour.

Dorothy

Well, we all knew it was coming. All those sandbags in Whitehall. And those silver balloons in the sky. I'm kind of relieved, to be frank. I found those last few months very hard to take.

Mrs. Roland

I'm sure so did we all. We've been through all this before, you know. You're too young to remember. We even had a zeppelin dropping bombs over London. When was it, dear?

Mr. Roland

In May 1915. Twenty-eight people were killed.

Dorothy

Really? I never heard of that.

Kenneth Lorimer arrives, *The Times* in hand.

Introductions.

Kenneth (to Dorothy)

I have admired you a few times in the lift. How do you do.

Dorothy (pointing to her towel)

I dressed up specially for you.

General laughter, welcomed by everybody.

Kenneth

Do you read *The Times*?

Dorothy

I'm afraid not. I'm strictly a *Daily Mail* girl.

Kenneth

I don't suppose the *Daily Mail* has done much better, but listen to what *The Times* says: "There is no answer in the end to the whole doctrine of force but force, and it will now be given with the determination, spirit and intelligence that can belong only to nations that have the right and the power to think for themselves."

Mr. Roland

What's wrong with that? Hasn't Mr. Chamberlain proven to the whole world that for us force is truly the last resort? If only we had applied it earlier! When Hitler started to rearm right after he came to power, for example, in breach of the Peace Treaty, and then later, three years ago, when he walked into the Rhineland. That's when we should have moved in.

Kenneth (shouting)

No, a thousand times no! At the first sign that he was tearing up the Treaty of Versailles we should have broken off all diplomatic relations with Germany and called a boycott of all German goods. At the second sign, we should have allowed the French to occupy the Ruhr again. They would have been only too delighted. At the third, the prime minister should have gone to Moscow, told the Soviets of our plans and tried to persuade them to cooperate with us. They may think the imperialist capitalist west is doomed but they don't like the Nazis any better than we do — and I bet you they still don't. They only made an deal with them to gain time and get a slice of Poland. When everything is said and done they would have preferred an alliance with us if we had asked them nicely, in good time. — Where was I? Ah yes, at the fourth sign, we should have stopped Hitler from buying oil — anywhere. At the fifth sign, we should have forbidden German planes from landing at our airports. At the sixth sign, we should have dropped thousands of leaflets over German cities telling the Germans what was going on in the concentration camps, because we knew all about it. But what did we do instead? We invited Herr Ribbentropp to wine and dine with us so that he could report to his boss we were only too anxious to play along with him.

Dorothy (to the colonel)

I think he's got a point, don't you?

Colonel
He does not. He doesn't have a clue of what Hitler's about and what the Germans are like.

Otto Koch, Ida Netter and Ludwig Heilbrunn arrive. There's only one chair free in the centre. Otto's mother suggests to Ludwig Heilbrunn that he take it. She and Otto preferred to sit in a corner with the other tenants and listen.

Colonel (cool and formal)
I am Colonel Reginald Thornton.

Heilbrunn
Dr. Ludwig Heilbrunn.

They bow to each other. The usual introductions follow.

Colonel
You must be very upset at the turn of events, Dr... what was it?... oh yes, Heilbrunn.

Heilbunn (his English could be better)
Not at today's events, colonel. But I would have been upset if England had once more tried to negotiate. We all know what's happening in Poland. One can hardly bear to think about it.

Mr. Roland
I find it surprising that you should say that, doctor. Aren't you German yourself?

Heilbrunn
I am a refugee.

Colonel
Did you fight in the last war?

Heilbrunn
As a matter of fact, I did not. I was an elected politician and was therefore exempted.

Mr. Roland
So you were an elected politician in the Kaiser's Germany?

Heilbrunn
Yes. In the Democratic Party.

Colonel (sharply)
Why didn't you become a refugee then?

Heilbrunn (stunned, highly agitated, stuttering)
The situation was very different. If you like, I can try and explain the difference right away.

Kenneth
Gentlemen, I don't think this is the time. We should not talk about such things while we can blown to bits at any moment. Nobody can think straight.

Dorothy
Speak for yourself. (Laughter.)

The sirens sound the "All clear." While all the tenants breathe sighs of relief, pick up their gas masks and leave, Kenneth and Dorothy go over to Ludwig Heilbrunn.

Kenneth
I want you to know that I understand your situation perfectly.

Heilbrunn
You do? Thank you. I am asking myself every day whether you English know what you are up against. How can you expect to win this war when you don't understand … how shall I put it? … the fundamentals?

Dorothy
I do.

Heilbrunn
You do?

Dorothy
Certainly. We English don't like foreigners.

Heilbrunn doesn't know how to respond.

Kenneth (putting his arm round Dorothy)
Exactly! You've hit the nail on the head. That's why in the end we will beat Adolf Hitler!

22

Sylvester

By the end of 1939 Otto's sister, Margo, and her husband, Paul, had their American visas and were in London, waiting for space on a ship to cross the Atlantic in a convoy. For the New Year's Eve celebration, they invited him to accompany them to a party held in a large flat in an apartment house in Hampstead, around the corner from 20 Maresfield Gardens where Freud had died three months earlier. The flat belonged to Oscar Wallach, an uncle of a school friend of Paul's from Cologne. Mr. Wallach, who himself stayed in the background, was a banker who had managed to transfer his money to England in good time and could easily afford to supply his nephew and his fellow refugees with seemingly unlimited amounts of champagne. This is why, if the celebrants had been able to remember the event the next day, they would undoubtedly have described it as the best *Sylvester*, the best New Year's Eve, they had ever had. Amnesia the morning after had always been considered the ultimate proof of a memorable celebration.

It was bitterly cold and the streets were covered with snow. The bus from West Kensington to Hampstead took ten minutes longer than usual. The Nazis had not yet dropped any bombs on London since the war had started nearly four months earlier, during what was beginning to be called the phony war. Still, the blackout regulations were being strictly enforced and London was pitch-black. This may have been unnecessary. Those who knew Germans had reason to doubt whether any of them were sober enough to fly on *Sylvester*.

In Oscar Wallach's crowded and smoke-filled dining room there was dancing to the sound of an excellent jazz pianist from Berlin and Paul had to raise his voice when he introduced Otto to his friends, Oscar's nephew Werner Wallach and his wife, Traute, who in turn introduced him to the girl of the evening, Jennifer Hill, an enchanting brown-eyed brunette, so far unattached, possibly the only English-born guest in the room. Otto could hardly wait until midnight — an hour away — to kiss her.

Her glass was empty.

"You look thirsty, Jennifer," Otto said.

"I am, desperately."

"I will put an end to this, come what may."

He looked around to locate the source of the champagne.

"You must feel rather lonely here, among all of us..." He searched for the right word. "...aliens."

"I rather like aliens."

She had a delicious smile.

Otto gestured amiably to a wandering refugee with a bottle and guided him to Jennifer's empty glass.

"You don't have much of an accent," she said. Otto knew this was not true but he was delighted to hear it. "How come?"

Otto explained the circumstances of his life, adding that he hoped that perhaps during the rest of the evening, she could help him get rid of what was left of his German accent. He said he knew of others who had not been in England as long as he had — nearly five years — who had got rid of it altogether. No doubt, with a lot of loving help.

"I will do my best. But if I were you," she said, "I would not wish to sound like an Englishman. A little touch of an accent will be of enormous help to you with the ladies. Look what Charles Boyer has achieved."

"All right. " Otto put his arm around her. "I will keep mine just for you. Let's listen. I love that song."

The pianist had just begun Cole Porter's "My Heart Belongs to Daddy." An acquaintance of Margo's sang it with a strong Stuttgart accent:

> If I invite a boy some night
> To dine on my fine
> Finnan haddie
> I just adore his
> Asking for more
> But my heart belongs to Daddy

When the applause had died down the dancing resumed. Soon Otto and Jennifer were dancing cheek to cheek.

After a champagne-stimulated countdown, it was finally midnight. To demonstrate an advanced state of acculturalization, the pianist played "The Lambeth Walk." Unlike all the other males — including Paul — who kissed every lady in the room, Otto stayed with Jennifer. It was truly remarkable what her tongue could do. The effect was earth-shaking.

"Jennifer," Otto stammered, "my heart belongs to you. Not to Daddy."

"You're not so bad either," she said.

No girl had ever paid him a greater compliment.

Soon food was served. Considering the rationing, it was sumptuous, especially the sardine savouries and the salami sandwiches made with margarine.

Their glasses were filled again.

A happy refugee from Breslau approached, a friend of Margo and Paul.

"Are you aliens?" he asked.

"Less so every minute," Otto replied, giving Jennifer a squeeze.

"I want to become alien," she said, swallowing another gulp of champagne. "How do I do that?"

"Hopeless." The man from Breslau shook his head sadly. "You can work on it as long as you like, young lady. You'll never make it. You happen to be at a terrible, terrible disadvantage. You're British. Sorry. Can't help you."

And he wandered on.

Jennifer and Otto went back to the dining room to dance. This time it was "Roll Out the Barrel."

After that they sat down, next to a man wearing a tuxedo and a red tie.

"What category are you?" he asked.

"C, of course," Otto replied.

"I could see it in your face," the man observed,

"Category of what?" Jennifer asked. "Male beauty?"

+++

Otto happened to be well informed on the subject of categories. He explained to her that at the beginning of the war the government established one hundred and twenty tribunals across the country to determine whether individual "enemy aliens" should be interned and locked up in camps right away or whether they could be exempted and remain free. Soon after the beginning of the First World War more than thirty thousand Germans (who had not returned to Germany) had been interned in an atmosphere of acute Germanophobia and spy-hysteria. But this time there were about seventy thousand refugees from Hitler's Germany in the UK, in addition to a sizeable number of German non-refugees. And there was very little Germanophobia. In 1914 no refugees from the Kaiser's Germany had come to England. Also, this time the government wanted to avoid mass internment, which in the 1914–18 war had led to much unnecessary suffering and was very costly.

So the government established tribunals to determine, in a calm and unemotional atmosphere, who was and who was not loyal to England. They were often headed by members of the gentry who had no legal training. On the whole, they did their job as conscientiously as they could with the means at their disposal, and they bent backwards to be fair. But they inevitably reflected the values of the society from which their members were drawn. This occasionally led to somewhat odd results. As far as Otto knew, however, they committed few, if any, gross injustices. The responsibility for the injustices that did occur, resulting in immediate internment, usually rested with the security organization MI5, not with the tribunals.

There was, for example, the case of Eugen Spier, a friend of Winston Churchill's who was now in the Cabinet as First Lord of the Admiralty. In the last few years Spier had seen eye to eye with Churchill and disapproved strongly of Chamberlain's policies. MI5 declared him a security risk and he was interned immediately.

There was also Bernhard Weiss, the social-democratic Jewish president of the Berlin police during the Weimar republic, who was the target of a particularly vicious propaganda campaign by Josef Goebbels. Weiss escaped and settled in England. At the outbreak of the war he was immediately interned together with a

Nazi whom he had arrested ten years earlier. When the mistake was discovered Weiss was released and henceforth treated like most other male refugees, i.e., interned in the spring of 1940 and later released.

The tribunals dealt with more than sixty-two thousand cases of Jews, half-Jews and non-Jews who still had German or Austrian citizenship. Among them, four hundred and eighty-six were considered security risks, put in Category A and interned immediately. In the cases of nine thousand three hundred and fourteen aliens, the tribunals could not make up their minds. They were placed in Category B. That meant, among other things, that they could not travel without police permission, had to stay away from airports and were not allowed to carry cameras. The remaining fifty-two thousand refugees could demonstrate their loyalty to England and were placed in Category C and were exempted from all restrictions.

Otto was among them.

✦✦✦

"What happened," Jennifer asked, "when you appeared before your tribunal in Cambridge?"

"The chairman," Otto replied, "looked at the dossier the Home Office had given him. 'Ah,' he beamed when the saw that I had gone to Cranbrook School. 'How's little old Pop?'"

Otto explained to Jennifer who Pop was.

"Pop was fine, as far as I knew," Otto said. "I hadn't seen him in a little while. The chairman said he knew about Pop from the son of a friend of his who went to Cranbrook. 'Did you make the First Eleven?' he asked. My heart sank. How could I tell him that I had never understood cricket?"

"Don't aliens play cricket?" Jennifer asked in mock innocence.

"They certainly do not! Let me go on. Would that condemn me to Category B? So I told him that I was a great batsman but perhaps not quite great enough. 'Never mind,' the chairman said with a benevolent smile. 'Even players in the Second Eleven can be loyal to England,' and he put me in Category C."

Traute Wallach, the hostess, appeared.

"I see you two are getting on all right."

"Not at all. " Otto pulled Jennifer closer to him. "This girl is far too bright for me."

"That's true," Jennifer said and kissed Otto on the cheek.

"Too bad," said Traute. "I've always prided myself on my match making. I hope I'm having more luck with my other couples."

"Now there's one thing I want to know," Jennifer said after Traute had gone. "Didn't you and your friends object to having to appear before a tribunal? After all, you were Hitler's original enemies!"

"True, of course, but it never occurred to any of us to object," Otto replied. "We are aliens in wartime. We are guests in a country that has been good to us. It is fighting Hitler."

"Not yet," said Jennifer.

An old lady with a double chin had been listening.

"It will," she said, "once it has lost a few battles and pulls up its socks. My name is Hildegard. What's yours?"

They told her.

"I haven't had such a good *Sylvester* since the Boer War."

"The Boer War?" they cried.

"What's so extraordinary about that? My father came to this country in 1901 to sell German leather. I was eighteen and in love with my piano teacher. So you figure out how old I am." She paused for a second. "Oh no, come to think of it, I had an even better *Sylvester* in the internment camp on the Isle of Man in 1916. And I wasn't in love with anybody."

"How strange," Otto said. "We were just talking about internment during the First World War."

"You were? Let me tell you." She addressed herself to Jennifer. "You British had gone completely crazy. You destroyed a perfectly loyal, well-integrated, peaceful and highly productive community that had evolved since the late nineteenth century. You saw a spy for the Kaiser under every bed. There was no sensible reason for interning more than a few dozen persons. The few spies the Kaiser may have sent over Scotland Yard could have found in five minutes, at any time. And put in existing prisons, not in new camps.

Anyhow, if the Kaiser wanted information all he had to do was ask his English relatives. Oh, the stupidity of it all! The Battenbergs had to call themselves Mountbatten. And Prince Louis, the First Sea Lord of the Royal Navy and the Earl of Mountbatten's father, was hounded out of office. But the yellow press demanded all of us be rounded up and put away. So the government obliged. It was convenient to have scapegoats."

"This time people are being more sensible," Jennifer observed.

"Yes, so far," the old lady said. "But if mass internment happened once it can happen again. If the conditions are ripe."

"Even for refugees?" Jennifer asked.

"Of course! Nothing easier than maligning them in the press. I could write the editorials for them: They're camouflaged spies. They take the bread out of our mouths. And they seduce the women away from our men."

"Oh no!" shouted Jennifer and poked Otto in the ribs.

"And most of them are *Jews!*" The old lady's double chin shook with excitement. "It's bad enough to be German — but to be Jewish as well! Obviously they've got to be put away. *For their own protection!*"

+++

For reasons that today seem inexplicable, I never saw Jennifer Hill again. When she kissed me good night she gave me her card, which I still have.

A recent internet search located many Jennifer Hills, one a television actress, born in Toronto, Canada, on New Year's Eve 1976.

23

Tea with the Master

Friday, March 1st, 1940

I have never had the impulse to keep a diary. I could never decide whether diaries are meant for one's own future use or for posthumous use by others. However, I am now going to try it. Momentous decisions are facing me. In a little more than two months I will be leaving Cambridge. I might as well try to keep a diary to record on paper the events leading up to that, and my responses to them. That may help me think straight. If it does I may continue afterwards.

For refugees in Category C, the Pioneer Corps [non-combatant units primarily for foreigners] seems be the only possible way to get into uniform. Before embarking for the U.S. with Margo to sail across the U-boat–infested Atlantic, Paul said I should consider following them and Robert to the New World rather than joining a "Battalion for Inferiors" in the Old. He told me I would be soft in the head if I imagined for a single moment that the English would ever accept me as an equal, even after I was naturalized. I replied that I had no illusions on that score but I felt more and more English every day, whatever they thought of me. And I added that for more than a century our crowd in Germany had felt more and more German whether the Germans accepted us or not. Of course, we thought they had. That may have been an illusion, as it turned out — mere wishful thinking. Too soon to say. I added with my customary worldly wisdom that one-sided love affairs were, after all, a common human experience and perhaps better than no love affairs at all. I said I had invested three years of my adult life in economics and law and I always did well in exams. Surely that was an asset that might miraculously lead somewhere.

In any case, how could I think about my future when I had my final exams to worry about? I did not mention the Koch jewellery business, which obviously would have to wait for my dynamic leadership until after the war. But I did say the obvious. It was a good thing, I said, that for the moment we did not have to worry about supporting Mother. Just before the war there had been an auction at Christie's of the smuggled antique watches, which had yielded enough to keep her housed and fed for a year or two. She was frugal by nature. So that was a load off our minds. It was hard for her to say goodbye to Margo and Paul, as it was for me, not knowing when, if ever, we would see each other again.

Tuesday, March 5th

I would never have thought that so soon after beginning this diary a major event would happen to test its usefulness.

Ten days ago students were invited to apply to the Cambridge University Joint Recruiting Board to be considered for a commission in His Majesty's Forces. I saw no reason why I should not accept this generous invitation and promptly filled out a form in which I stated, under the heading of "Nationality" that I was "German, i.e., a 'Refugee from Nazi Oppression,' fully exempted from special restrictions applicable to enemy aliens." I assumed that I would never hear from them again and forgot all about it. But then, last Thursday, I received a card asking me to appear before the Board this morning, at eleven o'clock, at Old Schools, near the Senate House.

I will never reveal to a living person what went through my mind when I received this card. Only this diary will know.

Do I really want to become an English officer? Do I want to learn how to kill and prepare myself to be killed?

Was I hesitating because I was a coward?

There is no question that I will do all I can to fight the Nazis. But how? Could I not meet my unquestioned obligation in some other way? Why did I not feel this was a Great Adventure? Obviously I would join up if I had to. But did I really want to *volunteer*? Why did I not feel the slightest urge to prove myself as a soldier, an urge that, from all accounts, my father felt most strongly in 1914?

Then another thought struck me with unexpected force: was joining the army very simply the price I had to pay to become an Englishman? But if the English would never accept me anyway, as Paul said, what was the point?

For the moment I let these questions hang in the air.

Then I asked myself another question. Suppose the Board were more intelligent than the Aliens' Tribunal last autumn. Suppose they asked me whether I would be prepared to kill the boys I had gone to school with in Frankfurt, some of whom had surely been my friends. I knew many of them only went along with the Nazis because they thought they had to, not out of any conviction. Could I really say in good conscience that this would not concern me at all?

Well, as it happened, I need not have worried. This was not a question I was asked.

We had a short, polite conversation. After that, the four men on the Board wanted to know only one thing:

"Do you have any preference in which infantry regiment you would like to serve?"

I said I did not.

They conferred for less than a minute.

Their decision was unanimous.

The candidate, they said, was eligible to be an officer in the infantry.

Wednesday, March 6th

Another test for the budding diarist. My reaction to the Recruiting Board's decision showed itself in a way no one, least of all I, could have predicted.

For this afternoon at five, E.A. Benians, the Master of St. John's College, invited a selection of professors and students, all members of the College, for tea at five. He did this from time to time. Now it was my turn. I had seen the Master at the High Table in Hall, and I knew he was an eminent historian of the British Empire. But I had never met him.

Nor had I ever been in the Master's Lodge, although I knew exactly where it was. I was now living in digs on 2 Richmond

Terrace, near the Round Church. But in my first year I had stayed in college, in A4 Chapel Court, on the east side of the river Cam. On the west side are the famous Backs, the pleasantly undulating lawns on which it is exhilarating to walk, and lie, and enjoy the sight of the amazing medieval buildings. The graceful Bridge of Sighs joins the sixteenth- and seventeenth-century College to the nineteenth-century New Court, on the west side of the River Cam. (It was literally a Cam-bridge.) The Master's Lodge was on the side of the old college, the east side, separated from my Chapel Court by the large Master's Garden bordering on the east side the river Cam.

Now it so happened that for some reason it was already pitch-black by four forty-five that afternoon. In the black-out, pitch-dark means pitch-dark. I was, of course, wearing my cap and gown — this was an academic occasion for which this was obligatory — and my gas mask. In short, I had to find the Master's Lodge across the Master's Garden in pitch-darkness.

Normally, had I not recently been declared competent to be a killer and to be killed, I would have had no trouble. I have a good sense of direction. But evidently this declaration had seriously upset my psychic balance. It seems that I now needed to prove to myself that the Recruiting Board was wrong and that I was, after all, unfit to be a British officer.

I was wise enough to avoid crossing the Bridge of Sighs, which would have led me to the New Court and the Backs. Quite properly, I remained on the east side of the Cam.

But I strayed.

I suddenly found myself in the River Cam.

I did not drown. I can swim. I climbed ashore. I was in no danger of being seen. Drenched and dripping I managed to run — no, to grope my way through the Chapel Court, through the Second and First Courts, and through the main gate to St. John's Street. It was so dark that even the eagle-eyed porter did not see me. Then northwards to my digs. I changed. Fortunately the student who lived above me was home and I could borrow his cap and gown. I kept the wet gas mask, probably useless now. A German gas attack was the last thing I was worrying about.

+++

Having saved myself so valiantly from an unscheduled baptism I was completely at ease and in excellent spirits when I offered the Master's wife my apologies for being twenty minutes late. I was forgiven, asked to sit down and offered a cup of tea. Two chemistry students arrived even later.

At the usual sherry parties, one stood up and wandered from one conversation to another. But at a tea party one sat down and there was only one conversation. Of the dons present I knew only two, the classics professor Martin Charlesworth, with whom I had friendly relations since he was a prominent member of the St. John's Musical Society, and Dean E.E. Raven, who once sat at my table in Hall.

When I came in the topic was the successful British boarding in Norwegian territorial waters of the *Altmark,* the German supply ship of the *Graf Spree,* which had been sunk in the River Plate in December. The *Altmark* was on the way back to Germany. Norway was neutral. In breach of international law, the First Lord of the Admiralty, Winston Churchill, had ordered the rescue of nearly three hundred British merchant sailors who had been on ships captured by the *Graf Spree.*

"As no one knows better than you do, Master," a venerable don with an untidy crown of white hair said with a smile, "the British Empire did not become great if the letter of the law had always been scrupulously observed."

"George, I will answer that mischievous observation only indirectly, if I may," the red-haired Master E.A. Benians replied. "Only last week I was reminded by one of our local papers that it was God's plan to use the British Empire as an instrument to bring about a better world."

We all laughed happily.

"Speaking of God," one of the two chemistry students reported, "my vicar got into trouble the other day for saying in his sermon at Evensong that God loves even Hitler."

"Oh, He does," Dean Raven responded. "I only assume it, of course, from all the evidence at hand. I won't pretend to have any first-hand knowledge."

Inevitably, the conversation moved from the excellent prospects of the Lady Margaret Boat Club to the perennial subject of the status of women at the university. This diary does not need not be told that they are not members and are confined to their own two colleges. Nor that we men generously permit them to attend lectures. Some one mentioned the old English scholar Sir Arthur Quiller-Couch who enjoyed taking a firm stand against women. He always arrived in the hall immaculately attired and began his lectures, which were very popular among women, with "gentlemen."

"I strongly sympathize with him," a debonair young don joked. "I couldn't find a seat at the University Library last Friday. It was full of women! Awful."

Then there were the obvious complaints about the evacuees from London — from Bedford College, Queen Mary College, the London School of Economics and so on — for whom college buildings had been requisitioned.

"Speaking of the Library," Martin Charlesworth said, "I hardly dare admit this in the Dean's presence but I had a moment of deeply un-Christian delight yesterday when I discovered there was nothing whatsoever to eat or drink left at the Library tea room, unbeknownst to the fifty or sixty hungry and thirsty London students queuing up."

"But Martin, how did you know they weren't our own students?" the Master asked.

"Instinct, Master," Charlesworth replied. "Instinct. One can always tell."

+++

When I got home I found a letter from Cecil H. Gorringe, the father of my friend John, who had invited me to his home in Amersham, Buckinghamshire, during the Christmas holidays a few weeks after Munich. Mr. Gorringe had become very upset when I suggested that another war was inevitable.

> Dear Otto,
> I should like to say how much I admire your courage and purpose in volunteering to join the Army. You have set an example for many of our young men who in my opinion

are not over anxious to make the sacrifice you have so willingly made.

But I can assure you that your action is appreciated and valued by all English men and women who would join with me in saying thank you. Perhaps in your spare odd moment you will find the time to let us know where and how you are.

I am afraid you will miss the quiet siesta after luncheon but there will be compensations.

With best wishes for your future and may it not be long before you are settling down again in that successful career.

Yours very sincerely,
Cecil H. Gorringe

24

A Precautionary Measure

Scene: Larry Hudson's Room, A20, Chapel Court, St. John's College, Cambridge.

Time: Saturday, May 11th, after dinner.

Larry and Otto are both facing law exams in two weeks' time. They arrive together in Larry's room, take off their caps and gowns and throw them on a chair. Larry is the son of Sir Arthur Hudson, a former Guards Officer, now attached to the Joint Intelligence Committee in Whitehall. Larry picks up a bottle of port and pours two glasses.

Larry
Look, Otto, this is very hush-hush. My father would probably kill me if he knew I'd spill the beans to you. I talked to him just before dinner. I couldn't tell you in Hall.

Otto
So they found out I'm a Nazi spy.

Larry
Come on, Otto, this is serious. I know you're not clever enough to be a Nazi spy but you'll be arrested tomorrow anyway.

Otto
Well, I admit that's quite interesting. Thanks for telling me. Do they know I'm Category C and that I am eligible to be an officer in the infantry?

Larry
They could not care less. Churchill had his first Cabinet meeting today at 12:30. The fourth item on the agenda was "Invasion of Great Britain." Everyone knew that the internment of aliens was bound to be raised. And it was.

Otto
With the result you just told me.

Larry
You don't seem to be very upset?

Otto
I've learned from you British not to show my emotions. All I can say is that the possibility of this happening had naturally already occurred to me. This is by no mean the worst thing for me. What about women? Are they going to intern my mother in London?

Larry
Don't worry. Only males between sixteen and sixty in the east and southeast will be rounded up at first, starting tomorrow morning at 8 a.m. Others, including women, may follow later. And don't ask me what to do about the exams. I know no more than you do.

Otto
I don't think I'll work very hard this weekend. But, on the other hand, maybe the way for me to get through the next twenty-four hours is to pretend to myself that you didn't tell me a thing.

Larry
Absolutely! What a wise old bird you are.

Otto
Yes, I know. So what happened in London? What else did your father tell you?

Larry
He told me that since the beginning of the war the Home Office had done everything possible to prevent a repeat of the mistakes made in 1914 — mass internment for the duration. That's the reason why they set up the tribunals. But now everything changed. Just a month after the Nazis conquered Denmark and Norway, they've attacked Holland and Belgium. Next will be France. Churchill has become prime minister and power has shifted from the Home Office to the War Office. It so happens that a report from the Joint Intelligence Committee

said that what the German fifth column had done in Norway — local Germans cooperating with the invader — could happen here. And who would constitute such a fifth column in England? The enemy aliens who were not interned, of course. That's the way they put it. And if you raised the point that most of them happen to be Hitler's first enemies, they would answer this is no doubt true but naturally that's exactly who Hitler's helpers would pretend to be.

Otto
Have they heard of any fifth columnist in Norway disguising himself as a Jewish refugee?

Larry
I have no idea.

Otto
Nor have I. But I doubt it. That's not the way the Nazi mind works. So Churchill said, "No more pussyfooting. Intern the lot!" I can hear him say it. Right?

Larry
I wasn't there. But I assume it.

Otto
Could he not have thanked the Home Office for having done such a great job anticipating events, setting up the tribunals and all that? Could he not have accepted their findings? England has always offered asylum to the victims of tyranny. Could he not have said that this is the kind of England we are fighting for?

Larry
Yes, he could have. And a lot of good people would have loved him for it. There certainly is no overwhelming, irresistible groundswell for the internment of aliens. True, several papers asked for it, but not fortissimo. Mezzoforte, I would say. There's no evidence that refugees are particularly unpopular. Or that they're considered dangerous. Except maybe in certain government departments in Whitehall. And there is no spy fever anywhere as there was in 1914. But, of course, no one knows how we will behave once the war really starts for us. If Churchill had said there are ways to protect us from

fifth columnists that would not involve the loss of liberty of thousands of Hitler's victims, everybody in the War Office would have said, "There goes Winston again, that old windbag. Back to his old tricks. He'll never make it." The War Office is not the Home Office. No, on his first day in office, he thought he had to be tough, grim and determined. He had to make it clear to one and all that the Chamberlain period was over. You'd better get a good night's sleep, Otto. Tomorrow will be a heavy day for you.

Otto
Why? I've already forgotten what you told me.

+++

I thought the cloudless day — Whitsunday, May 12th — would never end. Could the police have forgotten me? In a perverse way I was actually looking forward to being interned. It would solve a lot of problems. I would not have to be an officer. And if that wasn't in the cards after all, I would not have to look for a chance to do my bit in a civilian capacity.

I knew several other refugees and would have liked to compare notes with them but had been too busy swatting for my exams to keep in touch with any of them. Since George Mosse's departure for the United States, I was not close to any of them. In any case, thanks to Larry's father I knew more about what was going on than they did.

I packed a small suitcase with some essentials and typed a letter to my mother in London.

> ...Here we are all discussing what to do with parachutists. I was told that on Friday night when Chamberlain (did you hear him?) said "I have decided to resign" there was such a roar of joy in Trinity that no one could hear the rest of the speech.
>
> My exams start next Thursday week. I find it terribly difficult to work now, it's so futile. It is awful, awful. However...
>
> Love,
> Otto

I did not mail the letter, hoping that the police, once they came, would let me tell her what was happening, and drop it in a letterbox on the way to, I assumed, the police station.

For lunch I was invited at Newnham College (one of the two girls' colleges). There I was told there were rumours floating around that in the morning one or two "German citizens" had been "taken away." But nobody said they were refugees. So the girls thought I had no reason to worry.

When I returned to my digs, Mrs. Ripley, my landlady, told me, in a state of high agitation, that a policeman had been there *in a taxi* — could that have been true? — and asked for my nationality. She told him that she thought I was German. She then asked me, if I was a German spy and was removed, who would pay the rent for the next three weeks, which would be due on May 13? I told her not to worry, she would get her money. But she went on telling me she'd had no idea I was a German spy. I always paid my rent punctually and had never been a problem to her. So I said, this time rather sharply, I was not a German spy and she should stop talking nonsense, would she mind leaving me alone. And she did.

I added this to the letter to my mother:

> P.S. I was out for lunch today and when I came back I was told by my landlady that a policeman in a taxi had been there to ask for my nationality.

At last, at quarter past five, two constables in civilian suits arrived in an unmarked car, not a taxi.

After establishing my identity, the taller of the two spoke. The other remained silent.

"Sir, I am very sorry to have to ask you to come with me, please. Purely as a precautionary measure."

"I quite understand," I said. "I fully grasp the situation. But I have a big problem. My final exams are to begin Thursday week. Should I take along my notes and a few textbooks?"

"Oh no, sir," the constable said. "This is only for a few days while they sort things out in London. You can take along some notes if you like. But I would leave the heavy textbooks here. Just pack a pair of pyjamas and a toothbrush. You'll be back in good time for the exams"

"Thank you, Constable."

I went to my desk and scribbled a few words at the bottom of my letter.

> The police have just been here to fetch me (no idea where
> I shall go). I shall write as soon as I can, don't worry. In
> case we lose each other — Margo's address [in New York].

I sealed the letter.

"Would you mind terribly," I asked the constable, "if I posted this letter to my mother in London on the way?"

"I am sorry, sir. That would be against regulations. But don't worry. I will post it for you."

And he did. But before we left for the buses Mrs. Ripley wanted a quick word with him.

"Who do I turn to" she asked, "if this spy doesn't pay me the money he owes me?"

I wanted to say something appropriate but the constable was faster than I.

"Adolf Hitler," he said.

They drove to the site in front of the Senate House and Old Schools, on King's Parade, where the Joint Recruiting Board had pronounced me fit to be an officer in the British Army. Five large buses were waiting, and so were several dozen passengers-to-be, some of them quite elderly — one had a cane — each with a suitcase, calmly chatting with each other. Some were accompanied by girlfriends or wives. Police were everywhere. Most of the students and young professors wore their college scarves, as did I. I recognized not a single familiar face. Everybody spoke English. A few spectators had assembled to watch, neither friendly nor unfriendly. I heard somebody say that the BBC had reported the "rounding up" of male enemy aliens between sixteen and sixty all along the east coast.

I joined one of the groups.

"What are the rumours?" I asked.

"My constable said they would take us to a beautiful monastery in Ely," somebody said.

"Oh no," another trumped him, "mine said to an empty gym in the girls' school in Sawston."

It was getting dark when at last we were ready to go. There were about a hundred people in the crowd. The conversations about the latest news from Holland, from London, about exams, summer plans — even cricket! — were lively. Someone said the youngest son of the former Crown prince, one of the Kaiser's grandsons, was in one of the buses, under the name of Count Lingen. I had heard that he was in Cambridge.

Soon we arrived in Bury St. Edmunds, in East Anglia, about thirty-five miles north east of Cambridge. There the army took over. It was dark when we arrived.

We disembarked, were given straw pallets and herded into tents that had been put up in a field. There was nothing to eat or drink, but for many this did not matter very much as long as there were enough cigarettes and packages of pipe tobacco available. There were no latrines but the field was large.

A fellow prisoner asked me what I had been studying.

I said economics and law.

He took out a little book about Moscow's five-year plans.

"Read this," he said. "Stalin says when in jail you have to study."

25

An English Spring

"**K**och, I've been watching you," Mathias Landau said to me on our third day in Bury St. Edmunds. "You've got a lot to learn."

I had met Mathias once in Cambridge. I had no idea what he was doing there. All I knew about him was that he was the grandson of Paul Ehrlich, the Nobel Prize laureate for medicine in 1908, and the son of a famous mathematician. Also, that he was a Marxist and had fought in Spain.

"I've come to the right place," I responded. "I've already learned how to calculate the distances between the planets. On an empty stomach, too."

"Good for you, Koch. This may be the only useful thing you've learned so far. Because you've been listening to all the wrong people."

I had no idea what he had in mind. Apart from attending lectures on astronomy and the Byzantine mosaics in St. Mark's in Venice, I had been consorting with a history student from Berlin and a musician from Vienna.

"That may be so," I said. "But who are the right people?"

"All you need is me," Mathias declared with conviction. "It's no good listening to all those people who tell you what the Germans will do with us when they come. Such as line us up on the beaches and shoot us, *bang, bang, bang, bang*. That's not good for the nerves."

"I avoid them, too."

"And that man with the red beard who is telling everybody that the moment the Germans come we must stage a mass breakout and grab boats in the ports in the hope that a ship will pick us up."

"I have not heard him. Nor do I want to."

"Good. And what about that other man, the old classics professor, who said he was a Catholic and he was going to see the commandant and demand permission to send an urgent appeal to the Pope? Before the Germans come?"

"He didn't say that to me." I paused for a minute. "But, come to think of it, what's wrong with that?"

"Everything. You see, Koch, they're not going to come. After eliminating Holland and Belgium they will crush France. That will take no more than, say, one month. That's the moment when Hitler will propose peace to Churchill. By then the real fifth column will have done its work, some of them people who've been wining and dining Ribbentropp when he was here. They belong to the same clubs as Churchill, of course. They will have been in contact with the people around Hitler. These distinguished old friends agree that there is absolutely no point in fighting each other because, after all, they have a common enemy, the Bolsheviks. They should get together and fight them. And all top Nazis know that Hitler never intended to keep his agreement with Moscow, anyway. On that basis Churchill will accept Hitler's peace offer. After all, he's fought the Bolsheviks before, after the last war. It comes naturally to him. Of course the agreement to take on the Russians will remain a deadly secret — until it leaks out."

"Hm." I mulled this over. "Churchill may dislike the Bolsheviks," I said, "but he may dislike Nazis even more."

"Nonsense, Koch. He is guided by the logic of capitalism. People like you don't understand capitalism and its relation to the class system. To Churchill's class Stalin is a far greater threat than the Nazis will ever be."

"To Churchill's class, maybe," I wondered. "But to Churchill?"

"If he gets out of line," Mathias said, "the men in his clubs will dispose of him in no time. Lord Halifax is standing by, ready for the kill. Of course it will be done very politely, according to the rules of the game. After all, they're gentlemen. Just as politely as the way Churchill handles Chamberlain now. And certainly more politely than the way they're treating us, including a relative of His Majesty the King, Prince Friedrich of Prussia, who's here, as everybody knows, under the name of Count Lingen. He's in much demand, socially speaking. Have you talked to him?"

"I've looked at him, that's all. I don't push myself."

"Good. Now, what do you think that other, let me see, great grandson of Queen Victoria, the Duke of Windsor, and his lovely wife are waiting for?"

"I have no idea."

"Goering loves them and they love Goering. You figure it out. No, no, no. Hitler will win England without any invasion."

This demanded another short pause for thought.

"And once he's been given the keys to this camp," I asked, "surely he will line us up and shoot us — *bang, bang, bang, bang*?"

"If he can catch us. But by then clever men like you and me will be in New York and will read all about it in the *New York Times.*"

"And how will we get there?"

"By using our brains." Mathias smiled. "You just follow me. I found my way out of one of Franco's prisons — with some difficulty, mind you, but I managed it. This," he pointed to the elderly guards at the other side of the barbed wire, "is kindergarten stuff."

We stayed in Bury St. Edmunds for one week, cut off from the outside, unreachable by our families and friends. Nor did we get any news. We were not allowed any newspapers or wireless, with the result that the wildest rumours circulated in the camp, some no doubt fed by the guards. The news, Heaven knows, was bad enough without the guards' help. On Wednesday Holland surrendered and the RAF attacked the Ruhr. On Saturday Antwerp gave in, but Belgium did not surrender until May 28th. Mathias Landau's predictions were coming true. By then we were in our second camp.

We had been taken by train to Liverpool and deposited in an as yet unoccupied housing estate in the suburb of Huyton that was in its final stages of construction, with enough room for incoming internees from all over the country. By now internees were no longer arriving only from the restricted areas close to the eastern and southern coasts. The contractors' huts were still standing and there were piles of rubble everywhere. The estate was surrounded by a barbed wire fence seven feet high. Twelve men were allocated to each house. There was no furniture. Once again we were given straw pallets. We had cold water but no towels and not enough toilet paper. The Cambridge crowd stayed more or less together, but for the first time we met people very different from us, people most of us would never have met in our previous lives. The language spoken was German with its many dialects, including — this was very important — Viennese. We stayed in Huyton for three weeks, until Monday, June 10th, the day Mussolini declared war and twelve days before the French surrender. By then the evacuation of more than three hundred thousand members of the British Expeditionary Force and many thousand French soldiers at Dunkirk had been completed.

I first heard about this from Walter Loevinsohn, universally known as "The General," because of his lectures, both formal and informal, on military strategy. He was a chain smoker in his late twenties, had a bad leg and seemed to have excellent sources in the commandant's office. He was also a member of our governing camp committee. The commandant was a white-mustached veteran of the Great War who, when watching a group of internees with skullcaps and side curls who had arrived in the camp, was heard to say, "I had no idea there were so many Jews among the Nazis."

"No doubt," the general told me during an after-dinner chat, "the British will present the Dunkirk disaster as a splendid victory. But, Otto, not since the Boer War have they suffered such a smashing defeat. Much worse even than Churchill's personal disgrace at Gallipoli. But I must give it to them, it's an amazing achievement that they saved so many lives. I don't know how they did it. But it's bad news for us."

"Why, General?"

"Because nothing would have been easier for Hitler than to close the trap and destroy them. That was entirely within his power. I have looked at the map and I know the formations on both sides. He could have done it easily but he deliberately chose not to. Why do you think he refrained?"

"Because, General," I ventured, "he wanted to save his strength for the coming assault on Paris."

"No, Otto. For that he has more than enough. No, because he did not want to humiliate the British. He wanted them to know that they owe their survival to him, and to him alone. He wants them to be in a good pliable mood and grateful to him when he makes his peace proposal after taking the salute of his troops on the Champs Elysées."

I had an unpleasant feeling at the pit of my stomach.

"And will that strategy work?"

He used the butt of his cigarette to light the next one.

"Your guess is as good as mine," he said. "It may. Churchill, of course, won't negotiate. But the old appeasers may push him aside."

I did not want to ask him the obvious follow-up question: what happens to us if they succeed?

"Do you think, General," I asked instead, "there's any point in your committee discussing this with the commandant?"

"Perhaps. But not now. He's a decent chap who means well. Not before he recovers from the shock we inflicted on him at our meeting yesterday. He had made a statement that he thought was extraordinarily generous. He said he realized we were on different sides of the fence, we were Germans and he was English, but he would do all he could to make life tolerable for us. To that the Reverend Sommerville responded. Have you met him?"

I said I had seen him, an impressive looking elderly clergyman with a mane of white hair, but had never spoken to him.

"The reverend's speech was very simple. The men in the camp were German only technically, he said, in no other sense, even if they spoke German. Most of them were Jews who had been deprived of their rights in Germany. Many of them had been in concentration camps. No one had better reasons for fighting Hitler than the men over whom he had been put in charge. The commandant was stunned. This was entirely new to him, he said. He asked the Reverend Sommerville why he was here. The reverend answered with a sweet smile because no one had ever told him that he had to apply for English citizenship if he wanted to get rid of his German citizenship. He had an English father and a German mother who had met and married during an idyllic holiday in Bavaria before 1914. He had been born in Germany and was therefore a German citizen. But his mother had taken him to England as soon as she was fit to travel. He had lived all his life in England. His three sons were officers in the RAF. The commandant was shaken to the roots. He got up. He put on his cap, saluted the Reverend Sommerville and the rest of us, and marched out. No, Otto, we'll have to wait a few days before we can have any serious conversations with him."

Conditions in the camp improved gradually. The people outside the barbed wire, we told ourselves, did not have much more to eat than we did. However, there were differences. To test these, two of our enterprising young fellow-internees climbed through a hole in the fence to do some shopping. When they came back with the groceries they could not find the hole and promptly reported to the guard at the front gate. Of course, the guards wouldn't let them in. The two men were highly indignant. "But we live here!" they cried. The guards reluctantly yielded.

Once the camp was reasonably habitable, we were told that we were to be moved to the Isle of Man, half way between England and Ireland, and the place, we knew, where during the German internees had been interned for the duration of the Great War. The obvious explanation: Whitehall considered a German invasion imminent and wanted us potential fifth columnists out of the way. The idea that the Germans might wish to come via neutral Ireland and find us conveniently located *en route* had not occurred to them.

On the way to the port of Liverpool we had to walk a mile or two carrying our suitcases, not easy for the elderly. We younger internees helped them as well as we could. Some citizens, under the sad illusion that we were German seamen captured from German vessels by the British Navy, used unintelligible invective to speed us on our way. Some of us swore later that they spat at us. If so, I did not notice.

The British had put barbed wire around a row of requisitioned boarding houses in Douglas along the seafront, normally inhabited by holiday makers from England. That was the Central Camp. There were others, including one for women. Many internees who had arrived before us had already made themselves comfortable. The historian Moses Aberbach later wrote that "it is probable that the Isle of Man in the summer of 1940 was the greatest Jewish cultural and religious centre in Europe."

I was allocated to a house dominated by a voluble philosopher from Königsberg who had turned the name Hegel into the verb *hegeln*, i.e., to hegel, to talk and think the way Hegel did. Two of my fellow housemates were philosophy students and jumped at the chance. But for the rest of us it was heavy going. But I was more than compensated by the company of the tousle-headed pianist Peter Heller, a year younger than I, also from Cambridge, who looked like the young Beethoven. His father was a wealthy candy manufacturer in Vienna and his mother a writer of movie scripts. They had lived in the Berggasse in Vienna, next door to Freud. The two families were close. When Peter arrived on the Isle of Man he did not know that Freud's son, Martin, a member of the Royal Society, had also been interned and was probably somewhere on the island.

When Peter was twelve his parents separated. He had some minor symptoms, which others, in more innocent locations, would have ignored, but he became the first child patient of Anna Freud, who later made the psychoanalysis of children her life's work.

There was a pleasant promenade along the waterfront where we conducted our conversations. During one of these Peter asked me whether I recognized the quote, "The Jews are not the men who will be blamed for nothing."

"Hegel?" I tried.

"Wrong," he replied. "Jack the Ripper."

"How nice. Do you think the people in Whitehall are familiar with his collected works?"

"I don't doubt it for a minute." Peter paused. "Let me analyze your question," he continued after a moment's reflection. "You mean, do I think Jack the Ripper's observation was a factor in the decision to send us here? Was anti-Semitism one of the motives? If that is, indeed, your question I would say yes, definitely, but only in the sense that the entire non-Jewish world, which presumably includes Jack, is a little bit anti-Semitic."

"Yes, that is what I mean. It wasn't a major motive."

"You are speaking of normal anti-Semitism," he continued. "We all take that for granted. Maybe that is the reason why we accepted our imprisonment without a murmur of resentment. We say, first things first: the British are fighting Hitler, they are fighting our war for us, and everything else is secondary. Besides, submitting to authority, however unjust, is in our blood: we've been forced to do it since biblical times. We've always believed the important thing is what goes on within us and the way we live. I've even heard a rabbi say that the British had a duty to intern us. He said they would have been seriously delinquent if they had not."

"For Churchill's reasons? That you can't tell, and that some of us may not be what we pretend to be?"

"I suppose so." Peter pondered this. "Did it occur to you," he resumed, "that, since the British have confiscated our passports and whatever identification papers we may still have had, I can call myself Otto Koch and you can call yourself Peter Heller and nobody could challenge it?"

"I prefer the name Schickelgruber," I said.

At that moment Prince Friedrich von Preussen, the Kaiser's grandson, accompanied by a staff of Cambridge courtiers, was strolling along the promenade towards us and suddenly faced us. By now I had met him and, apparently, so had Peter.

"Good morning, Mr. Koch," the prince said to me.

"Good morning, Mr. Heller," the prince said to Peter.

"Good morning," I said.

"Good morning," Peter said.

We continued our promenade. We both had no idea what to call him. His courtiers called him Fritz, but the two of us were too proud to have joined that group. We could not call him "Your Royal Highness" because the Kaiser had lost his throne in 1918 and we were democrats. Nor could we call him Count Lingen, even if that was one of the dozens of titles on his birth certificate and the name he was using for the time being. That would have been too easy and too prosaic for us.

"Is it not strange," Peter asked, "that I was enormously pleased that Fritz greeted me by name?"

"So was I," I confessed. "I can hardly wait to tell him that my father was his grandfather's court jeweller and that we had lying around the house drawings His Majesty made for a tiara to be given to the prince's grandmother for her birthday."

"I am duly impressed," Peter said. "Now let us analyze that. What are the subterranean reasons for our shameless snobbery?"

"He's every inch a prince," I mused. "A fairy-tale prince. The anointed prince of our dreams." And so he was — blond and blue eyed, gallant, modest, polite, a little aloof. But generous. We knew he shared with his courtiers the parcels he received every week from Fortnum and Mason, which his relatives in Buckingham Palace ordered for him.

"May I submit," Peter said, "that we also have Jewish reasons. We are amazed when a true prince seemingly overcomes his normal anti-Semitism and treats us like human beings."

"Yes, this is an entirely new experience for us," I said. "Very gratifying. As to his grandfather, all I can say for him is that in his day many of us Jews became rich. Whatever he thought of us. Probably the same unflattering things as everybody else. Of course, he had a few Jewish friends, but only rich ones. Who knows what goes on in Fritz's head when he is so polite to Mr. Rosental and Mr. Aronsohn?"

"Now, since we are in an analytical mood, I have another little problem," Peter said as we approached our Hegelian House. "How come we can discuss such matters so calmly when all rational signs point to Hitler taking over England and, therefore, this camp, one way or another, will soon be in his hands and that we will all be sent to a large concentration camps near Lublin in Poland, perhaps as soon as, say, Friday week?"

"Why are you asking me?" I said. "Surely, the disciples of your adoptive father Sigmund Freud have the answer. Something — is it lack of imagination or ordinary stupidity? — makes it impossible for us to believe it. In our hearts we know that we will survive Adolf Hitler."

When, a few days later, we were struck by dysentery on board the S.S. *Ettrick* on our way to Canada, although we were never told where we were going, we were too sick to care whether we survived him or not.

On June 29th, one week after France's surrender, I had written to my mother, "This may be my last letter from Europe. The rumour about Canada seems to be materializing. All we know is that those between twenty and thirty shall leave the Isle of Man for an unknown destination. [The next few words were blacked out by the censor.] This letter is written on the assumption that we shall leave soon ... We will have to do work 'that appeals to us' (the officer said so). What that means we don't know. I am prepared to do anything, go anywhere. The chance to get to the States seems considerable..."

Two days after I wrote that letter we were shipped back to Liverpool and taken to a large hall. Lists of those selected to go overseas — ostensibly only unmarried men under thirty — were put up. The selection process was chaotic. Those who wanted to go could easily switch names with those who did not. I have not heard of anybody who actually did this, but one has to admit it was a fine idea in theory. A number of men, far older than thirty, chose to go. Nobody objected. Fathers who wanted to go with their sons were allowed to do so. Henry Kreisel, from Vienna, was sixteen. All he wanted to do in life was write poetry. His father, who was interned with him, objected vehemently. He wanted him to learn a respectable trade. Naturally, Henry tried his utmost to stay away from his father so he could write in peace. When it was announced that young people could go overseas he was overjoyed. At last he would be liberated! He had not heard about fathers being allowed to come along. One can imagine the shock when the poor boy spotted his all-too-caring dad on deck after both had recovered from dysentery. Later, they were reconciled.

The *Ettrick* was an eleven-thousand-ton troopship, built two years earlier. It had just evacuated a number of people from St. Jean de Luz, including King Zog of Albania, and was now to carry one thousand three hundred and eight internees in categories B and C, seven hundred and eighty-five German prisoners of war and four hundred and five Italians, far beyond its normal capacity, to a destination presumably the captain knew. The passengers only guessed it was Canada. The prisoners of war, mostly in uniform, were given by far the best accommodation. The officers had cabins on the top deck. All of them, officers and men, were, after all, clearly protected by the Geneva Convention. Few of our people talked to them but I heard of one of us who met a schoolmate.

Barbed wire had been strung along the walls of the *Ettrick.* We slept in hammocks below deck, crammed in like sardines, without ventilation. During the first few days we were not allowed on deck. If a torpedo had struck our chances would have been nil. On the second day out we heard whispered rumours that this is exactly what happened to our sister ship, the S.S. *Arandora Star*, which had sailed a few hours before us. The rumour was accompanied by the urgent advice not to talk about it to anybody, to avoid panic. But panic was the last thing on our minds when, on the same day, dysentery broke out and long, interminable lines formed outside the toilets. It had become impossible for most of us to contain the eruptions from both ends. On the way to the toilets one had to wade through oceans of liquid excrements and vomit. The stench was suffocating.

For some reason our prince and his Cambridge courtiers had been spared and they were (unlike me) in the best of health, as was Hans Kahle, one of our older men, an impressive-looking, pipe-smoking, straighforward professional soldier who as a graduate of the *Kadettenanstalt* had become an officer in the German Army in 1918 at the age of eighteen and become a communist after the war. He had been commander in the Eleventh International Brigade in the Spanish civil war and a character in Hemingway's *For Whom The Bell Tolls.* Our prince, his Cambridge courtiers and Hans Kahle got hold of rubber boots, brooms, buckets, brushes and formed what was to become the legendary Latrine Brigade. They got hold of enough Lysol to clean things up and procured paregoric to cure us. Within a day or two they earned the eternal gratitude of all of us who were stricken and a place in history.

We were weakened and thirsty but exhilarated as we entered the Gulf of St. Lawrence, in glorious weather, on the tenth day out of Liverpool. It could no longer be concealed from us that this was Canada. Soon villages with church steeples came into sight and even human beings, Canadians. We were full of hope. What kind of work did they have in mind when they promised us that we could do something useful at last? One boy from Berlin sang *Wir fahren jetzt nach Kanada — da war noch kaana da* ("We are now approaching Canada, nobody has ever been there"), an atrocious pun on the word Canada, and, as we sailed along the shoreline, one of our students gave us a lecture on Canadian history. Nobody listened.

Naval vessels appeared from nowhere and accompanied us as we approached the Rock of Quebec, a stunning sight. Once we landed at the foot, in Wolfe's Cove, the entire Canadian Army and Navy seemed to be there to welcome us, strongly supported by the entire Royal Canadian Mounted Police. After waiting on deck for some hours in the burning hot sun, during which a few us fainted, we disembarked. Prisoners of war were separated from us, and so were the Italians, whom we had never seen on board. Buses, heavily guarded and accompanied by motorcycle escorts, drove us up the Rock of Quebec to the Plains of Abraham, in the centre of the city. A crowd assembled as we stepped off the buses, amazed that some of the Nazi parachutists, or whatever they had been told we were, had disguised themselves as high school boys, bespectacled professors, bearded rabbis and rabbinical students with traditional earlocks. One captain heard some of us speak English and was heard to say to another, "Yes, yes, I know. Those are the most dangerous ones."

We were taken to a barracks while our luggage was being "dealt with." Anything we had on us, such as money, watches, cigarette cases or pen knives, was impounded and entered on official sheets. None of it was ever returned. Behind our backs, some of our luggage was looted. After all, since time immemorial soldiers have looted enemy property. A few months later, the Army conducted a series of courts martial, but none of us got anything back. From me they stole a rusty nail file, a comb from Woolworth's and a pack of cards. When one of us complained that he had been deprived of a bottle of aspirins, he was told, "Never mind. In Canada you won't get a headache."

When all this was over, we moved to Camp L, on the Plains

of Abraham, with a gorgeous view of the St. Lawrence, near the Citadel, the summer residence of Canada's Governor General, the Earl of Athlone, the younger brother of Queen Mary, and his wife Princess Alice, a granddaughter of Queen Victoria, who happened to be our prince's godmother.

The commandant was Major L.C.W. Wiggs, a pleasant, well-meaning Quebec coal merchant, soon to be nicknamed "Piggy Wiggy." A few hours before our boat arrived he was flabbergasted to receive a call from Princess Alice, around the corner in the Citadel, requesting him, please, to be so kind as to tell the dear grandson of her first cousin, who was to be his guest, that she had called.

The day after we had settled in Piggy Wiggy appointed our prince camp spokesman.

26

The Kaiser and I

On May 10th, 1940, Hitler's army invaded Holland. The former Kaiser Wilhelm II, at the age of eighty-one, was living in exile in Doorn, between the advancing German troops and the Dutch defensive forces. Three and a half hours after the Germans crossed the border, the Dutch commandant sent word that he and his suite were to consider themselves interned. They were enemy aliens. The Dutch were unlikely to have known that after launching his attack Adolf Hitler had sent a letter to Wilhelm inviting him to come to whatever place in Germany he might choose, a letter that the Kaiser's second wife, Hermine, a member of the minor Prussian nobility and thirty years younger than he, had described as "handsome and worthy." He had married her in 1922 after the death of the *Kaiserin*. One is free to speculate whether Hitler was playing with the idea of a highly implausible reconciliation with Wilhelm and, almost unthinkable, a possible restoration of the monarchy.

Up to now, Wilhelm's surrender and defection in 1918 had made him anathema to Hitler, who was very much aware that many Germans were nostalgic for the good old days. Moreover, Hitler knew that any dissident general might, at any time, wish to play politics with the ex-Kaiser. That is why he gave orders that, once his troops had occupied Doorn, there was to be no fraternization between the *Wehrmacht* and the former Supreme War Lord. A special attachment was to be posted at the gatehouse to prevent such contamination.

As to Wilhelm, his attitude towards the Nazis was far from consistent. On the one hand, he had followed the progress of the German military since April with sympathy and approval and was proud that one son and eight grandsons were serving in the German

Army. On the other, a year and a half earlier, after Munich, he had declared in a letter to Queen Mary — his first communication with a member of the English royal family since 1918: "No doubt Mr. N. Chamberlain was inspired by Heaven and guided by God who took pity on His children on earth by crowning his mission with such relieving success, God bless him."

That letter was consonant with the nausea he felt when he read about the *Kristallnacht,* a month after Munich. However, he showed his own more refined style of anti-Semitism in December 1940, in a letter to his friend Alfred Niemann, when Hitler seemed to be winning the war. The British elite, he wrote, with their Hebraic and Masonic satellites, had played one power off against the others. Now the day of reckoning had arrived. Britain's future lay in cooperating with German-dominated Europe and not with the United States. To another correspondent he wrote that the British upper class was poisoned and completely ruled by Jewry.

May 11, 1940, the day after the Nazi assault on Holland, was Churchill's first day in office. Hitler's troops had not yet reached the Kaiser's villa, though gunfire could be heard in the distance. After clearing it with the King and the Foreign Secretary, Lord Halifax, Churchill sent a message through the embassy in the Hague to the mayor of Doorn, Baron van Nagell, asking him, please, to convey to the Kaiser and his wife in the name of the British government an offer of asylum in England. If he accepted an RAF plane would land in Holland within hours to pick them up.

One can imagine the scene. It was late in the evening. Wilhelm was in a dressing gown, reading, downstairs. Hermine had already gone to bed. The Dutch had interned four of his five servants. The remaining one was fast asleep. The doorbell rang. Wilhelm had to open the door himself. Baron van Nagell was standing there. He announced he had an important message from London. The Kaiser said, "Please come in" and offered him a seat in the living room.

Hermine emerged from the bedroom.

"What is it, dear?" she called down.

"You'd better join us."

The Baron relayed his message. They listened calmly and requested a little time to think it over. "Of course, Your Majesty," the baron said. He would be back in the morning to receive the answer.

The answer was "No thank you." The British ambassador promptly reported to London: "Offer of asylum gratefully declined."

In a letter to his daughter, the Kaiser explained that he considered the British offer a temptation from Satan. It was a piece of impudence, he believed, a propaganda move by Churchill. He would rather be shot than flee to England, where he would be forced to be photographed with his old nemesis. The brilliant leading generals in this war came from *his* school, he wrote. They had fought under *his* command in the Great War as lieutenants, captains and young majors. The old Prussian spirit, the spirit of Frederick the Great, had manifested itself once again.

At the moment the message declining the offer of asylum arrived at the Foreign Office, at 6:51 on the evening of May 12, one of Wilhelm's grandsons and I were in Cambridge outside the Senate House, waiting for the buses to take us to Bury St. Edmunds. We had been arrested shortly before at Churchill's orders. If the Kaiser had known that, it would have given him an excellent additional reason.

The next day, to Wilhelm's jubilation, the *Wehrmacht* entered Doorn, the Kaiser's servants were freed from internment and he ordered that champagne be served with dinner.

+++

On June 4th, 1941, Wilhelm died. In accordance with his wish to be buried with his ancestors in Germany only if the monarchy was restored, his final resting place was in Doorn. Among the hundred and seventy-one wreaths sent for the funeral was an arrangement of lilies in the valley and orchids sent by the Führer.

Hermine went back to her estate in Silesia. In 1945 it was taken over by the Soviet army. She died in penury in 1947.

+++

The question arises why our prince, who, like his brothers, had served in the German army — in fact, he was with the *Wehrmacht's* tank corps when Germany occupied Austria in March 1938 — did not return from Cambridge to Germany in September 1939 to participate in the war. The answer is not clear. Assuming that the entire Hohenzollern family in various degrees considered Hitler a vulgar upstart, the brothers reluctantly came to terms with him in the absence of a more attractive alternative. Our prince thought the more attractive alternative was a future in England. It would be tempting to say that he had more integrity than the others — tempting, but possibly wrong. His oldest brother, Prince Louis Ferdinand, was involved in the plot against Hitler in July 1944, risking his own life. In short, I don't know the answer.

Let us examine the evidence. Prince Friedrich of Prussia was born in Berlin in 1911. In the 'thirties he played a role in Berlin's diplomatic society. The daughter of the American ambassador, William E. Dodd, referred to his "air of shy innocence and guilelessness" in her memoirs. "If he had a mind at all unique or interesting," she wrote, "I was never privileged to see it ... and I think my experience was not uncommon. But I had never seen a prince before and certainly never a handsome, blushing one." Later, some of those who were close to him in camp and greatly respected and admired him came to a similar conclusion. They thought he was a thoroughly decent person and certainly a committed anti-Nazi but that he was "not very bright."

Prince Friedrich came to the United Kingdom in 1937 to study banking at the House of Schröder in the City. After serving with the *Wehrmacht,* in Austria in Mach 1938, he returned to England and became an undergraduate in Cambridge to be tutored by the historian George M. Trevelyan. He was not a great student and seems to have been preoccupied with the question what to do with his life, not an easy question since at that time it seemed likely, if not probable, that Hitler would start a war that he might very well win. Where would the prince fit in? Early in 1940 the home secretary, Sir John Anderson, told the House of Commons that the West of Scotland tribunal had granted the prince an exemption from internment.

His life after internment does not throw any more light on his motivations.

In December 1940 he returned to England and was released. After studying agriculture he set up a model farm in Hertfordshire, near Bishop's Stortford, between Cambridge and London. In July 1945 he married Lady Brigid Guinness, of the beer family, the youngest daughter of Lord Iveagh. They had three sons and two daughters. In 1953 he adopted the title Prince Friedrich of Prussia. In the spring of 1961 his wife sought a divorce. A date was fixed for the hearing.

On May 1st, 1961, his body was found in the Rhine, after a ten-day search. He had been inspecting his vinyards at Schloss Rheinhartshausen near Bingen. It was assumed that Prince Friedrich had committed suicide. According to his brother, Louis Ferdinand, he had been suffering from nervous depression. No details were given.

27

A Love Story

Nature was prodigiously generous to us. The view from our camp of the valley of the St. Lawrence below, and of the villages with their church steeples on the other shore in the distance, was glorious. It provided the perfect backdrop to the tender love story I am about to tell. Everything around us was sumptuous. The St. Lawrence was mightier than the Rhine and the Danube combined, not to mention the Volga, the colours brighter, the sunsets more intensely blood-red and the thunderstorms noisier than those at home. And we soon found out that our camp was located on the Plains of Abraham, the only world-class battlefield in Canada, where in 1759 the English beat the French and the future of Canada was decided. This made us feel as important as though we had been incarcerated on the battlefields of Waterloo or Gettysburg.

There were two walkways along the barbed wire and watchtowers surrounding the camp, one close to the compound and the other twenty meters, a shouting distance, away. Curious Quebeckers could stroll along the outer walkway and inspect those of us who happened to be visible, and if they shouted we could hear them, and vice versa. Of course this, or any other communication whatsoever between them and us, was strictly forbidden.

One such curious Quebecker was Pauline Perrault, a blond school girl of fifteen who lived in her grandfather's house on the Grande Allée, the most fashionable street in Quebec. The grandfather was the Liberal Senator Charles Alphonse Fournier, a friend of Mackenzie King's, and noted for his resemblance to Sir Wilfred Laurier. He doted on her. Pauline's parents were separated. Her mother and aunt also lived there.

It so happened that our camp was on the route between the Grande Allée and Pauline's school. So, by making only a small detour, she could focus her attention on the man of her choice — Peter Field.

Pauline had good taste. Peter looked like a Wagnerian tenor — handsome, blond, imposing. He was *old*, twenty-six, and came from Vienna. He had been a book salesman in Germany, Poland and Holland before the war. From Holland he made a hair's-breadth escape, only to be interned in a Liverpool barracks, in his words a real "hell hole." But he didn't mind. He was amazed he was still alive.

By September, a time when the leaves were just beginning to turn, and the valley of the St. Lawrence was golden brown, and several of our poets were polishing their sonnets in praise of the Canadian autumn, the relationship between Pauline and Peter had matured from an exchange of amorous blown kisses to an exchange of amorous notes — and more. All this began with the help of one of the guards who had been watching.

"You like Blondie?" he had asked Peter one day. "She enquired about you."

At first Peter did not believe him. He thought the guard was teasing him. But then the guard wanted to know whether he would like her name and address. Peter said yes, of course. If he'd get it for him he would give him his penknife.

This was quite a change from the occasion when he had shouted hello to Pauline. A guard, not the same guard, had him arrested and thrown in the clink for a few hours.

This time the helpful guard told Peter a few days later that he had the address and threw a piece of paper at him. Peter picked it up and dropped the penknife on the same spot.

Not long afterwards we were moved to Camp N in Sherbrooke, three hours away by train. A regular correspondence ensued. (The French Canadian girl's English was better than his.) I did no know Peter well at the time, but we later became friends and he told me many things I did not know at the time. It was easy for me to understand that Pauline developed a schoolgirl's crush on

Peter. After all, what is more romantic than a handsome prisoner languishing behind barbed wire? It was just as easy to understand that Peter was immensely amused, and flattered, by her attention, especially since it had begun as a public entertainment.

But it was not quite as easy to understand that he would become serious. Well, he certainly did. This was not a mere flirtation. At one stage, he told me, and no doubt everybody else, that he would write a letter to the commandant asking to be let out, just for a few hours, on his word of honour, and be allowed to visit the girl. He said he would go mad if the commandant said no.

He did not write the letter and he did not go mad, or rather not more mad than the rest of us whose mental health had also been grievously undermined by not having a seen a live woman, except on the distant, outer walkway in Quebec City, since May. He did not write to the commandant but, now that he had Pauline's address, wrote to her, and she wrote to him, many times. The censors must have enjoyed reading the torrid letters. She sent him photographs of herself, posing on the monuments of generals Wolfe and Montcalm, the fallen heroes of the Battle of Quebec.

Many months later, more than a year after Pauline had first blown a kiss to him, it finally became possible for friends, relatives and others to make arrangements to visit us. By this time our camp was among the three that, at last, had been named "Refugee Camps."

In due course, Pauline, her mother and aunt came from Quebec City to Sherbrooke.

"About eight hundred guys," Peter refreshed my memory of the scene later, "pressed their noses against the barbed wire to watch the scene. She did all the right things. She ran towards me, fell into my arms and kissed me. She loved every minute of it and played it up to the hilt. The men just howled. We must have been together for an hour or so. They had brought me so many packages that someone had to get permission to come with a wheelbarrow to cart them into the camp."

Peter made a good impression. The two ladies asked Pauline's grandfather in Ottawa to pull a few strings to achieve something that was absolutely unheard of, something that up to that moment had been unthinkable, that Peter visit them in Quebec over a weekend. It is not clear whether the grandfather's friend Prime Minister Mackenzie King had a hand in this, but permission was granted. Peter was allowed to proceed from Friday October 3rd to Sunday October 5th, 1941.

"I was asked to sign that I would be back midnight on Sunday," he reported later. "At the time the place was full of rumours that we would be released soon. I was very much aware that I was sort of a test case, and that if there was trouble, if I was late coming back for example, everyone would suffer.

"As far as money was concerned, I had a hundred dollar bill that I had saved from Holland. I kept it hidden in my little bag. Wearing my one and only suit, I was driven to the railway station in Sherbrooke. Never having lived as a free man in an English-speaking country before, the mere experience of asking for a ticket in English was entirely new to me. It was amazing."

Pauline was at the station with her mother and aunt. There was great jubilation.

"They took me to their apartment and soon dinner was served. After dinner Pauline and I walked to a drugstore. I had a sundae, my first black and white sundae. Then we went up the roof of her apartment house where we sat around and necked. I was surprised that her mother allowed her to be alone with me.

"On Saturday morning Pauline came into my room wearing a negligée. She did not make it easy for me, but I behaved like a gentleman. She was a very precocious city child, sixteen going on twenty-one. We went out, exploring the city. I bought a dark blue suit, very much like a bar mitzvah suit, using thirty of my hundred dollars.

"On Sunday evening, they saw me off at the station. On arrival in Sherbrooke I hailed a taxi. 'To the internment camp,' I said to the driver, very much aware of the bizarre nature of the situation. I arrived early, just after ten o'clock, but the lights had already been turned off.

"It was incredible. Everybody came rushing out of their bunks. They shoved me into a top bunk and shouted 'Speak!'"

"Salivating collectively, they demanded graphic details.

"Not a single person believed me when I told them the truth."

+++

A few months later Peter was released. He visited Pauline several times but without a barbed wire between the two lovers the romance was doomed.

28

Sherbrooke

September 17th, 1940, Camp L, Quebec City
Another momentous change is afoot. It's time to fish out my diary from the bottom of my beaten-up old suitcase under the bed. I forget all about it when we have only routine excitements. I have no urge to record the attempted putsches against the lawfully elected hut-governments or the conducted tours (conducted by heavily armed tour guides) along the Grande Allée when we walk four in a row, like convent girls. Piggy Wiggy is proud of his city and wants to show it off. But before proceeding to record the Great Change to come, I will now say farewell to Camp L in my own fashion.

After the two months of under-nourishment in the English camps the food, Canadian army rations, prepared by our own expert cooks, is terrific. And the army barracks — huts we call them — in which we live are perfectly adequate. We actually sleep in beds.

Clearly, we have no right to complain.

But complain we do — endlessly. Our complaints are all variations on one theme, the non-comprehension by the Canadian military to grasp who we are. It does not matter how often we state the obvious, it will not sink in. Their misapprehension was dramatically demonstrated by our reception in Quebec. Piggy Wiggy has a heart of gold, and no doubt he believes what our prince tells him. (It is endlessly entertaining to watch the theatre provided by him and the prince not knowing who should salute whom.) But Piggy Wiggy is not the problem. His superiors in Ottawa are. They think they are doing their job conscientiously looking after us to help the government of the mother country, which, at a time of great danger, wanted to unburden itself of enemy nationals on its soil.

Once we were Piggy Wiggy's guests three interesting questions arose. For the record, let me recapitulate.

1. Should we agree to wear the POW uniform they provided — a blue denim jacket with a large red patch on the back and blue pants with a red strip down each side? We refused. After long debates, we changed our minds and gave in.

2. Regulations provided that we were to write our weekly one-page letters or postcards on POW paper. We refused. After long debates we changed our minds and gave in.

3. Should we accept the good offices of the International Red Cross, or the Swiss consul who reported to the German government?

After long debates we refused. This time we did not give in.

Before deporting us, the British had promised us — verbally — that we would be allowed to do useful work at our unspecified destination. But by now they had other things on their mind than request the Canadians implement their rash promise. So we consoled ourselves by finding work, or at least absorbing activity, in two ways, by establishing a "Popular University" and attending it, and by conducting scrupulously democratic debates at our interminable hut meetings. Of course, in our spare time we are free to play with the football that our prince's godmother, Princess Alice, had sent to our camp.

Only about sixty percent of the inhabitants of Camp L are Jews. The others are non-Jewish political refugees, and Nazis (presumably in Category B) whose primary home is Hut 14. They believe in the *Führerprinzip*, not in democracy.

This mix is just right for many exquisite exercises in applied political theory.

Should there be proportional representation in the senior meetings, with Nazis represented in accordance to their numbers, as "innocent" Piggy Wiggy requires?

Should the Nazis be allowed to participate in the activities of the Popular University if they promise not to talk about politics?

Is Hut 14 to be allotted the same number of tickets as all the other huts for cabaret performances in the dining hall?

What rights should be granted to a specific Nazi who is writing a book about an obscure subject without any access to libraries?

When challenged, he said "Adolf Hitler, while in prison, wrote the greatest book of the century, *Mein Kampf*, without any access to libraries."

Enough of all that. My diary is, after all, reserved for only Really Big Happenings.

Such as the one to come.

It is getting cool. The Geneva Convention doesn't allow the Canadian military to let its guests freeze to death. Only the dining hall can be properly heated. We have been told we will be split up and moved to other camps, perhaps merged with others, before the snow falls. Lists are being drawn up. We are ordered to put down our religion. Could it be true what we hear, that Protestants will be separated from Catholics? There are persistent rumours to that effect. Not just Jews from Gentiles. With that distinction, using a somewhat different vocabulary, we are only too familiar. One hopes the people here have never heard of the Nuremberg Laws. Separation between two different branches of Christendom? Why? And what about half-Jews? Half-Christians? What about quarter-Jews? Quarter-Christians? Agnostics? Atheists? If there are two or three destinations, and if space is a problem, are there no easier criteria? Why not just use the alphabet? Or the colour of hair? Or create a special camp for football players?

Max Perutz is a great science teacher at our camp school. He shows his students how to unravel the arrangement of atoms in crystals. Max is nominally a Catholic. He will do anything not to be separated from his friend (sorry, I always forget his name — let us call him Fritz) who is nominally a Protestant. Before the war, they had climbed mountains and gone skiing together, and shared girlfriends. Max wants to stay with the Protestants because apparently they are to be joined to the Jews. There are many scientists among the Jews. Max wants to be with them, never mind whether they are Jews or not. Anyway, I think at least one of his grandparents was Jewish. So after a surprisingly short search, Max and Fritz found Albert, a nominal Protestant who for his own reasons wants to be with the nominal Catholics. Assuming that rumours predicting something unpleasant usually turn out to be true, Max and Albert have decided to change identities. Max says, "We're just like the two swains Ferrando and Guglielmo in *Cosi fan tutte.* So what if we are unmasked?" he asks. "Will we be expelled?"

If so, let's all do it!

October 16th, Camp N, Sherbrooke, Quebec
This is what the diary is for. High drama at last!

Heaven only knows how they eventually made their distinctions. In this camp there appear to be mainly Jews and a few Protestants, seven hundred and thirty-six of us altogether, including our prince. Presumably no Catholics. The evidence? Max and Albert have been separated. Albert and Fritz are very pleased with themselves.

Yesterday, three hours in the train. The landscape — drab, utterly uninteresting. It is raining. We had already had some snow in Quebec, but it didn't stay on the ground.

Suddenly the train stops. The guards tell us we have arrived. We descend. This is not a railway station, we observe. But what is it? There are two sheds of some sort. And pits running through the sheds, filled with black water, along railway tracks. Soot is everywhere. The windows are broken. The roof is leaking. There is no sign of beds. In the so-called kitchen, army rations are waiting to be prepared by our expert cooks. We discover a few low-pressure water taps. No shower facilities. Six lavatories and two urinals, for use by seven hundred and thirty-six Jews and an unknown number of Protestants. No doubt the Catholics, we say, have more than enough gold-plated showers, lavatories and urinals in their "Heaven" to accommodate the world's entire Catholic population!

Could the rumour be true that the real reason we were evicted from our Garden of Eden was to make room for Nazi prisoners?

We decide, at a noisy gathering outside the sheds, in a kind of schoolyard, that we have no choice but to go on a hunger strike until we received assurances that we will forthwith be sent to a habitable camp. When I say "we" I mean the most vociferous of us. The matter is not put to a vote.

My own behaviour is admittedly far from admirable. I watch and listen from a distance, a few meters away from the excited crowd, feeling — what? superior? cowardly? too stupid to come up with a better solution?

Our prince does not want to be camp leader any more. The new leader, soon confirmed by the commandant, is Hans Kahle, the defender of Madrid.

He forms a committee consisting of Bruno Weinberg, an experienced international lawyer who has spent many years in Geneva with the League of Nations, two or three of our many doctors, one eminent architect, and our camp rabbi, Emil Fackenheim. (We actually have two, but Emil is the more eloquent.)

This morning, on an empty stomach, they meet with the commandant, Major S.N. Griffin. Poor man! None of this is his fault! There is no sign that he knows he is dealing with royalty.

I was not present at the meeting. But I can imagine what happened.

Kahle introduces his committee.

Weinberg rattles off the clauses in the Geneva Convention and other laws the Canadian government has flagrantly infringed by dumping us here. He also tells Major Griffin that British Ministry of Health prison regulations require a minimum of thirty-five square feet for each prisoner. He had quickly calculated we only had twenty-nine.

The doctors point to the stagnant water in the ditches and announce we are all going to perish in the very near future as a result of deadly diseases spread by the insects breeding there at this very moment. The architect says this place is unfit for human habitation and simply cannot be fixed up. And Rabbi Fackenheim declares that if we are left here all believers, Jews and Protestant alike, are doomed to lose their faith in no time at all!

Major Griffin assures the delegation that he is doing all he can to improve matters but that at this moment he is unable to give them the assurance we are asking for. He tells them that his Assistant Adjutant, Second Lieutenant J.A. Edmison, has asked for permission to speak to the internees and, after listening to what he intended to say, he, Major Griffin, had given permission, on condition that it was understood by one and all that he did not speak for the major him but only for himself.

October 17th

I was too tired last night to write down what Second Lieutenant Edmison said, standing on a table top in the schoolyard. He is certainly the first Canadian officer we have met who really does seem to understand our situation. But just because of that he threw some of us (including me) totally off balance, not merely because we were hungry.

He seemed to be a nice man, well educated, smooth, a Montreal lawyer and alderman, in his late thirties. No doubt he meant well. He said he was well acquainted with the Jewish community in Montreal. He was an honorary member of B'nai Brith and active in the Society for Christians and Jews. Before the war, he said, he had taken a strong anti-appeasement position. He said he had taken the trouble to find out exactly who we were. He knew there were many people among us who had been in concentration camps. He had every sympathy for our complaints. He considered them completely legitimate. But he assured us they would be taken seriously only if we cooperated. If we continued with our passive resistance we would inevitably be the losers, no one else. Above all, we should not expect any help from the Jewish community in Canada, which was concentrating on trying to persuade the government to admit refugees from Europe who were much worse off than we were. This was an uphill battle. There was much opposition to it. The one thing the Jewish community would most definitely not support would be Jews who were, after all, safe, rocking the boat. "So — please cooperate!"

I found this an appalling argument, and so did many of my friends. We all accepted as sincere the officer's declaration of sympathy with our position. No doubt he meant well. But he spoke as a lawyer, pleading the case for the military, a political lawyer at that, using any argument he could think of to break our will. We were not living in Canada. Nobody ever suggested there was the slightest possibility of any of us ever being released in Canada. To tell us that by fighting for our rights, which he indirectly admitted were being denied to us, we were undermining the case the Canadian Jewish community was making for helping our fellow Jews in Europe was profoundly unfair, a hit below the belt. He was connecting two situations that were unconnected. True, some of us, no doubt, had written letters to Jewish organizations in Canada during the summer, complaining about our plight, but we all understand that the British interned us and only the British can get us out. We were, as it were, on British territory. The Canadians were merely caretakers for the British, and were not doing a very good job of it, at the moment. Piggy Wiggy had done a good job. But that seemed long, long ago. In short, we had no relation to the Canadian Jewish community. This officer was speaking to us as though we had.

We held a meeting. Those who thought along these lines were in a minority. The majority decided we should give up our passive resistance immediately and give them three days — until midnight October 19th — to make arrangements to move us to a habitable camp.

Then we adjourned for lunch.

In the afternoon, one hundred and eight men from Camp Q, near Monteith in northern Ontario, arrived.

October 18th

One day before our deadline.

In the morning Commandant Griffin spoke to us in the yard. To indicate to us how seriously he took the matter, he had written out his speech and read it. He was the first to admit, he announced, that there was much to be done to improve conditions in the camp. If we worked together, we could perform wonders. Then he made his declaration. Sherbrooke is not going to be a temporary camp. "You and I are going to be here for a long time!" Then he made his direct appeal to us. We would get twenty cents a day for everything done to improve the camp. The only unpaid work would be for ordinary fatigues.

"There are among you many clever and qualified men," he declared. "To them I throw out the challenge to assist in the planning and erection of this new camp. You will tell me what materials you need and I will supply them without delay ... The winter is fast approaching and every day's delay is serious ... Please stop talking and arguing. I speak to you not only as commandant

171

but as man to man. I hope a lot of things will be different from now on."

When he finished he handed his written speech to Kahle.

Good, but not quite good enough, the camp decided. In any case, at the very least, we would have to be moved elsewhere while the camp was being made habitable. The newcomers from Camp Q wrote a formal letter to the commandant saying that he did not seem to be sufficiently aware of the gravity of the situation.

Whatever good Major Griffin had done was seriously endangered by another officer who suddenly appeared on the scene, Major D.J. O'Donahoe, a tall, red-faced Colonel Blimp. He also addressed us in the yard outside one of the two sheds. Immediately after his speech I went to a corner and wrote down exactly what he said.

Do you all understand English? (Yes.) You are here in custody. If you are asking for trouble you can have it, and plenty of it. I have had very bad reports about you. Do not try any more monkey business. You will have to carry out every order you get. We have ways and means to make you do it. This fellow needs a haircut. (Hear Hear!) You are all Jews here. (Yes. No.) Well, that's all right. But you've got to wash, otherwise you get lice. We did not put you here. You just happen to be here. If you play ball, I will play ball. If you don't pay ball, I won't play ball. That's all there is to it. I am not threatening you. I am simply stating facts. We are here to teach you fellows discipline. We have got nothing to do with your internment. We are only your custodians. Can you hear me? (Yes. No.)

You want us to win the war? (Yes, yes, yes.) We are going to start right here. Will you help? (Yes.) You are going to be asked — no, you are gong to be ordered — to work, first woodwork, second netmaking. Do you all understand that? (Yes. No.) Some of you have been in the business of making things. Well, we will teach you something useful so that when you get out of here by the end of the war, the time you have been interned will not be entirely wasted.

This (he pointed to the shed) is going to be your home. (Laughter.) And you will have to keep it clean. Some of you may have a certain grade of reasonable intelligence, so you won't misunderstand kindness for weakness. We'll get you machines.

Are there any people here who know how to make furniture? Joiners? Woodcutters? Tailors? I want to have a word with them.

November 10th

I have not made an entry for three weeks. I broke off the last one a little abruptly, I notice, after the speech by Major Balls, the man who wants to play ball with us. The situation became too confusing for me. Those who wanted to resume our hunger strike after midnight October 19th insisted they were prepared to resist to the last man a combined assault of tanks and heavily armed Canadian troops storming the compound with fixed bayonets, with every intention to mow us down. However, they easily gave way to the Voice of Reason. In other words, we caved in. Good thing that the commandant turned out to be as good as his word. Within three days armies of plumbers, carpenters and electricians arrived, with carloads of building materials, blowing the wind out of our sails. Of course, the Army knew far better than we did what was required. The speed with which they, with our help, for twenty cents a day, drained and covered the pits, installed new windows, fixed the roof and constructed a coke-fired hot-water system with showers, toilets and wash basins left us breathless. If we had moved elsewhere while this was going on we would have been deprived of an amazing experience. How fast they build things in the New World! No doubt skyscrapers do not take much longer! In no time the kitchen was ready to accommodate the many chefs and pastry cooks among us, each claiming to have worked for the Ritz and the Savoy, not to mention the Café Sacher in Vienna. Major Balls, too, delivered. Machines soon arrived to equip several workshops. Those of us who want to make money hammering munitions boxes, sewing kitbags or knitting nets can do so. I have a chance to make enough cigarette money to meet my needs holding a rope, standing firmly on the ground, while others risk their necks standing on ladders high up in the dining hall, putting in finishing touches on the new ceiling.

November 20th

Oh horrors! Four days ago our two swains, Ferrando and Guglielmo in *Cosi fan tutte,* were unmasked. I never found out how. Max

Perutz was summoned to appear before the commandant. Major Griffin, he reported to us, was impressed by the purity of his motives but nevertheless convicted him to three days in the local prison. They locked him up in a cage resembling a monkey's in a zoo. No chair, no bed, only a wooden plank. He had hidden some books inside his baggy plus-fours — they didn't want him to wear his POW uniform — so he was far less bored than the guard who had to march up and down on the other side of the iron grill. His sleep was interrupted only by the occasional drunk. He was in excellent spirits when he came out today.

The sergeant major gave him a big welcome. Ah, the sergeant major. He happens to like Max. I think he also likes Klaus Fuchs, who teaches physics in the camp school with Max. Klaus is silent, pale and bespectacled — I think he's the son of a Quaker, and probably a Quaker himself, a courageous opponent of Hitler. Klaus comes from Rüsselsheim, near Frankfurt, is very left wing and gets on well with our pipe-smoking camp leader, Hans Kahle who is a proud communist. But Kahle is more jovial than the austere Klaus. For all I know, Klaus, too, is a communist. I am told he is a superb physics teacher. He's not in my group and lives in a world far from mine. We've never talked, but we've stood side by side several times during roll calls. For that matter, I have no personal relations with Kahle either, just as I didn't with our prince, who is now very much in the background, protected from the mob by his Cambridge courtiers, playing bridge most of the time. I am told he does not play very well.

Max and Klaus are lucky to be in the sergeant major's good books. His regime is totally arbitrary. He governs by bellowing. (He has bellowed at me several times for not making my bed properly.) He's the tsar of all works programs, so naturally I keep out of his way. His name is Macintosh and he's a big, red-faced bully with huge bags under his eyes and a tiny mustache right under his nose. He has told his favourites that before the war he was a used car dealer in Sherbrooke and hopes to be one again after the war. He is a Canadian patriot and boasts that he can't stand the British. (His origin is Scottish.) He does not understand why anybody would want to fight for them unless ordered to do so. He makes no bones about disliking Jews. No anti-Semitism is harmless but, compared to the Nazi variety, his is noisy but touchingly innocent and without an ounce of malice. And, of course, totally ignorant. Last week he asked one of our sixteen-year-olds who he knew was not Jewish why he hung around "with all those dirty Jews." The boy replied that in a largely Jewish camp he had no choice. But, anyhow, the Jews were not dirty but very fine people. "After all," he added, "Einstein is a Jew." "Einstein, Einstein?" the sergeant major asked. "What group is he in?"

November 28

I have been getting letters regularly from Mother in London, which I am of course keeping. All that needs to be said here is that I worry a lot about her even though she assures me that she usually goes downstairs to the basement when there's an air raid. But the last letter really shook me. The *Arandora Star* was the *Ettrick's* sister ship. She left Liverpool a few hours before the *Ettrick* and was torpedoed off the Irish Coast. Nearly six hundred internees, mostly Italians, drowned, but also at least fifty-three anti-Nazi Jewish and non-Jewish refugees. But there were many survivors. All this I knew. But what Mother wrote me this time she had never written to me before, namely that for two interminable days in early July she assumed, on the basis what had been indicated to her by the Home Office, that I was likely to be among those lost.

The British public was deeply shocked by the sinking of the *Arandora Star.* Up to that moment it had not been widely known that anti-Nazis had been deported and put at risk. Now there was universal condemnation. In mid July there was a heated debate in Parliament. The government was put on the defensive. Soon they started releasing internees from the Isle of Man and from other camps. A week ago, Mother wrote, the Home Office sent a commissioner by the name of Alexander Paterson to Canada to interview internees and decide whether they might be eligible for release in England under various categories, but primarily whether they were willing to serve in the Pioneer Corps. (I've already heard rumours to that effect from others.) Now she is very much afraid that I might go back and join the Pioneer Corps, for the obvious reasons that I am safe in Canada and would not be safe in England. But it's not only that. She is terrified of torpedoes. With good reason. Her friend Kurt Stern went to England from Italy just before the war. I remembered him from our visit to Florence in 1938 when we had to listen *Rigoletto* in Italian. He was interned and released. In late August he drowned on the way to New York on his second attempt. After his first, a few weeks earlier, he was rescued. His wife, Gemma, and their little son had gone before him and were waiting for him in New York.

December 10th

I've had a terrible, agonizing week of indecision. I was constantly changing my mind, day and night. Now it's over, for the moment at least. Paterson was here for two days, interviewing candidates willing to return to England. I was not among them. But most of my Cambridge friends were. So, for now, the matter has been resolved. But we are told he will be back, to recruit a second batch. I'm not going to worry about that now, especially since he has told several of my friends that he is intending to proceed to Washington, on behalf of the British government, to see whether those of us who have first-degree relatives in the U.S. could be admitted.

I did not want to give any of my Cambridge friends a chance to lecture me on my obligations. I preferred to resolve this by myself. There was not an argument in favour of going back that I did not think of myself, above all that I had a moral duty to do my bit and that I wasn't doing my bit sitting in an internment camp being bellowed at by the sergeant major. Paul's argument that the Pioneer Corps was a unit for people the British did not trust was nonsense: it was obvious by now that one could graduate from it into the regular army. This raised the ancient question: did I really want to be a soldier? If I chose to stay I had to accept that, unless Paterson persuaded Washington, it was entirely possible, if not likely, that I would have to stay in this camp "for the duration." The war was going abominably...

And then there was Mother...

Evidently Paterson is a nice man who has spent his life reforming the British prison system. It is bitterly cold right now but he does not wear an overcoat. He doesn't believe in wearing overcoats, he says. Two of us knew him before the war. Walter Wallich met him in Berlin during a school holiday (he was going to an English school like Cranbrook) through an English journalist he knew. Paterson was attending a prison congress at the time. He met Ernst Bornemann in London, in connection with a film about prisons on which he was working, in which German prison experts were somehow involved. Paterson recognized them immediately. They had long talks. He confided to them that he doesn't think much of the military characters he had met in Ottawa. He didn't bring with him any notes and made all the decisions — life-and-death decisions for those involved — on the basis of his impressions alone.

December 20th

Paterson worked fast. Those who have been chosen have been notified. They may leave for England at any moment. Several farewell "parties" (no alcohol, of course) are proceeding simultaneously, with speeches and lots of bravura jokes. I will have to say goodbye to most of my Cambridge friends. Very painful. They say there will soon be another opportunity for me "to see the light."

Among those leaving — our prince, Hans Kahle, Max Perutz and Klaus Fuchs.

+++

In 1962 Max Perutz received the Nobel Prize in chemistry, with John Kendrew, "for their studiesin the structure of globaular proteins." He died in 2002.

In 1950 Klaus Fuchs was convicted for communicating atomic secrets from the United Kingdom to the Soviet Union. After serving nine of fourteen years in prison, he was released and allowed to the German Democratic Republic, where he continued his scientific career. He died in 1988.

29

You'll Get Used to It

August 10th, 1941
Dear Robert,
First of all, congratulations on your new job. The prospect of
visiting you in New Orleans isn't quite as remote as it was last
time I wrote, but it won't be tomorrow. Yes, I know Quebec and
Louisiana have a lot in common. I've been reading the American
history you sent me. Our Goethe Gymnasium should be heavily
reprimanded for teaching us almost none of this. All I remember
learning about North America is that Quebec had something to
do with Frederic the Great and Louisiana with Napoleon. Now,
thanks to you, I know everything.

Your description of the night life in the *vieux carré* makes
me salivate. It is certainly more amusing than the nightlife in
Camp N, where the sergeant major, who is also the guardian of
heterosexual morals, has trained his men go along the aisles,
flashlight in hand, to make sure that there is only one internee
under each blanket, both in the upper bunks and in the lower
bunks. (We have double-decker beds.) Our bedroom (Shed A)
houses about eight hundred men, who all snore, but not in
unison so that there is a constant sawing noise. If the sergeant
major's snoops find double occupancy they chase the guest
out. The absence of women has induced quite a number of us
to stray, but so far I have remained faithful to my memories
of conventional love objects and I am keeping myself pure for
new ones to come, sooner I hope rather than later. Someone
said the other day that if in one year from now we're still here,
the sergeant major will have to ask Ottawa for reinforcements
because by then we will all have succumbed. I have reason to
hope that I won't be able to participate in the experiment.

I don't know whether I'll have space to answer all your questions even though we are now allowed fifty lines a letter, thanks to our camp having been baptized "Refugee Camp" on July 1st. However, if we want to write even longer letters, the censor won't object if we use the allotments of friends who have nobody to write to. That is what I have done in this case.

Since I've just mentioned the censor I might as well begin with your second question, the painful drama about that letter of mine Margo wrote to you about. Fortunately it all ended well. I admit I was an idiot to write the things I wrote. I don't know how much she told you. Let me summarize. On July 12th I wrote a highly depressed letter. We had just been told, after our hopes had been raised again and again, that emigration to the Unites States was, after all, impossible. (I have already thanked you for arranging the affidavit for me but, if you insist, I'll do it again.) I wrote that I didn't expect the improvement that came with our new official status as refugees would amount to very much, that I was afraid new rules about working would cut into my spare time, which I needed for my legal studies — please note that for the moment I have abandoned any idea of being able one day to resurrect the Koch jewellery business, and that, since the possibility of release in Canada appeared to be non-existent, I had intended to go back to England with the next batch. Nobody should tell Mother: there was no need to worry her about my crossing the Atlantic. I was going to surprise her once I arrived. In England I hoped to be released in one of the civilian categories rather than having to "yield to a recruiting officer." That phrase enraged Paul (who, however, is still against my joining the Pioneer Corps) nearly as much as the reason I gave for it, namely that I was "really a civilian at heart." (I will comment on these statements below.)

The censor underlined the offending passages and sent the letter to his boss, Lieutenant Colonel R.S.W. Fordham, Commissioner of Refugee Camps, who sent it on to Margo and Paul. He pointed out to them (they sent me a copy of his letter) that these statements were "either untrue, improper or unfair" and went on to say that it was "sometimes very difficult to make certain refugees comfortable and happy in any sense of the word as instances occur where they seem anxious to find fault or complain, and it is feared that the present example is such a case. Actually, many changes have been made of late for the benefit of Refugees, and it is probably correct to say that nowhere are they treated better than in Canada. When Mr. Koch writes a letter of this character he incurs the risk of having the question of his allegiance adversely viewed. Nevertheless, the letter is being forwarded to you rather than withheld, and the writer is being asked to be more careful in future about what he puts on paper."

Quite rightly, Margo and Paul were greatly upset, but not as much as I was, because the suggestion that the attitude revealed in my letter raised a question of my allegiance had to be taken most seriously. The implications were obviously horrific. After raising hell with me they suggested I should write a letter to Lieutenant Colonel Fordham setting things straight, pointing out to him, among other things, that the Cambridge Recruiting Board had decided I was officer material and that, of course, I was willing to serve in the British Army. Which I did.

What followed was truly remarkable.

You may remember my descriptions of Pop, my house master at Cranbrook who is a dwarf but an intellectual giant. It so happens that he has a brother, Jack, an eminent economist high up in the British High Commission (the embassy) in Ottawa. Pop wrote to his brother about me, hoping that he and his wife, Honour, could do something for me. So, a few days after the letter incident, they met Lieutenant Colonel Fordham at a dinner party. Jack Osborne told him that one of his brother's former pupils, Otto Koch, was in his care. Fordham recognized the name immediately. He probably also mentioned my letter. In any case, a week or two later, when he visited the camp, I was called out to meet him. Of course, I feared the worst. However, there was no need. On the contrary. He turned out to be an affable, agreeable man, a lawyer himself, and a human being as well. He confirmed what had already been rumoured in the camp, namely that a possible release in Canada, under one category or another, may, after all, not be entirely impossible for us, some time in the indeterminate future. One category was for students but they had to be under twenty-one, which leaves me out. There was certainly no category for lawyers. "Lawyers in wartime are an unnecessary evil," he said. "I am a King's Counsel myself, and I have dropped my practice for the duration. You should learn something useful." I said I hoped to take a course in draughtsmanship, "Very good, very good," he said and the interview was over. I think he had me called out only out of curiosity. He did not mention the Osbornes. They wrote to me about meeting him only afterwards, when they confirmed what I already suspected — that, after this had been cleared with the British government, our fate was now entirely in Fordham's hands. It is he who will have to decide, when the time comes, whether I can be released in Canada, provided a Canadian could be found to assume the necessary financial, legal and moral responsibilities as "sponsor."

You will have to admit that the idea that such a time may one day come is a tremendously important step forward. I think it would be rash of me to think that it will come any time soon. But the doors to Canada are opening. This puts to an end all my agonizing dilemmas and has made all the difference in the world to my morale. I have no doubt sooner or later, one way or another, a sponsor can be found.

Now, let me explain, if not justify, my letter. I have now been behind barbed wire for sixteen months while momentous events are taking place in the outside world. There is no doubt that the long enforced isolation has turned us all (in various degrees) into self-centred, self-pitying navel gazers. Obviously I no longer judge correctly how the things I write in my letters strike those outside. To have written to Paul, of all people, that I really was a civilian at heart was sheer stupidity. Of course, so is he, and so are we all. How could I have done such a dense thing? It must sound as though I was not willing to honour my undoubted obligation to do all I can to fight the Nazis. What I meant, of course, was that there may be non-military ways of fighting them, more effective ways perhaps, than to be a not very competent cog in a great big military machine. I try not to think

that this is a mere rationalization of cowardice, though of course
it may be. I would not be at all surprised if many honourable
people are asking themselves the same question but are more
diplomatic than I was in the way they formulate it on paper.

Now to your first question. Yes, I am together with
many people whom I would never have met under normal
circumstances. Many are light-years removed from our crowd in
Frankfurt, as are your comrades in New Orleans, no doubt. This
makes me realize every day what hopelessly narrow lives we
used to live.

I am together with men who want one to believe that they
were members of the underworld, which may or may not be
true. They must be distinguished from proud members of the
proletariat. Why should all Jews be urban middle class? Of
course, most of us are but by no means all. Are you wondering
where the communists fit in? Well, if you think that our
communists are mostly proletarian you would be wrong. They
are largely middle class. Proletarian or middle class, some of
them take the view that if a member of their group receives gifts
by mail — money, tobacco, food — these should be shared from
each according to his ability and to each according to his need,
whereas non-communists usually consider such a sharing as gifts
or loans to be repaid if and when feasible. We also have a few
orthodox Jews, but most of them are in the camp in Fort Lennox,
on the Île aux Noix, not far from Montreal. Last November
Ottawa decreed that they are required to perform certain duties
on the Sabbath (such as, I imagine, making their beds), because
in Canada the Lord's Day Act defines Sunday as the Lord's Day.
(As far as I know, Christians don't object to making their beds
on Sundays.) "Refusal to do so," the regulation threatened, "may
result in charges being laid, which will be the subject of judicial
action." Jewish organizations were mobilized. Eventually Ottawa
relented. There was similar trouble about the orthodox Jews'
dietary requirements.

Let me go on. We have any number of odd characters in the
camp, a few wrestlers, one strong man who can carry a grand
piano on his back (so he says), one *Muskelzwerg* [muscle dwarf]

who is also a Jiu-Jitsu champion. His amazing physique enabled him to survive all kinds of horrors in Dachau. We have one professional juggler and one escape artist, universally known as *Klettermaxe,* who tried it and was caught. We have a few farmers, a sprinkling of sailors, many artisans, bohemians, poets, architects, doctors, artists of many kinds, actors, academics of all stripes, one violin virtuoso who practises in the boiler room, one psychoanalyst from Vienna and one Jew-for-Christ. Most of us are under thirty. Among the older ones the majority is engaged in commerce. My social group is that of students, not specifically Cambridge students, severely depleted since last December. The Cambridge crowd was widely denounced as arrogant, snobbish and offensively British. The common language spoken in the camp is German but they spoke English.

In the list of odd characters I nearly forgot to mention Baron von Ketschendorf, who refuses to wear the POW uniform. He insists on putting on stiff collars, silk shirts, spats and polished shoes. He has bushy eyebrows, carries a walking stick and never forgets to put on a monocle for the roll calls (twice a day).

But I must not mislead you. There is danger in dwelling too much on the theatrical aspects of our condition: comic characters, anecdotes, funny stories. Many of us are deeply depressed. There is much acute suffering. People worry about their families. Life without women is hard. Even though I try hard to stand aside and look at it all as theatre I, too, have occasionally lapsed into periods of self-pitying lethargy. I mean — the absurdity of it all! Until my interview with Fordham there was no end in sight — the only chance to get out of here (other than returning to the UK) seemed to be emigration to the U.S., and Jewish organizations constructed all kinds of schemes to make this possible, via Newfoundland or Cuba. Margo spent a lot of time on this, too. And we are only a mile or two north of the American border!

But now we may have reached a turning point. Who knows? By Christmas I may be a free man in Canada.

There was another turning point: June 22nd, when the Nazis tore up the Ribbentropp-Molotov Pact and attacked the

USSR. That took a huge moral burden off the shoulders of our communists. I have a Marxist friend, Heinz Kamnitzer from Berlin — he worked with Brecht at one point — who is terrifically bright. He says even if at first Hitler scores a number of victories he is bound to suffer the fate of Napoleon. He also predicts that sooner or later you Americans will come in. He says now, at last, the end of the war is in sight. He may well be right.

In the meantime, we are here and have no choice but to make the best of it. Our camp song helps. It was composed by Freddy Grant, who used to work with Gladys Fields in London:

> You'll get used to it.
> You'll get used to it.
> The first year is the worst year —
> Then you get used to it.
> You may scream and you may shout
> They'll never let you out!
> It serves you right, you so-and-so —
> Why aren't you a naturalized eskimo?

Love,
Otto

30

The Summit

I owe my release to Oscar Wilde.

The Dublin-born Sir Edward Carson (1854–1935), later Lord Carson of Duncairn, had his first success at the English bar in the criminal libel action brought in 1895 by the Marquess of Queensberry against Oscar Wilde. It made him England's most famous advocate. If he had fluffed the case and been forced back into Irish obscurity he would not have been able to send Edward (born in 1920), the son of his second marriage, to Cambridge. Edward became a friend of Hans Netter, the son of a cousin of Emil Netter whom I saw frequently.

In the late summer of 1941, my mother in London asked everybody, among others Hans's mother, Cecile, a cousin of Emil Netter's, whether they knew anybody in Canada who might be persuaded to sponsor me. Cecile put the question to Lady Carson, the mother of Hans's friend, who happen to know Gerald and Phyllis Birks in Montreal. Gerald was the son of Henry Birks, the founder of Canada's most prestigious jewellery firm. She wrote to them, mentioning that I was the grandson of Robert Koch, the Birks of Frankfurt. Yes, of course, they wrote back, they would be pleased to follow this up.

On Monday, October 27, I was called out of the compound by the commandant. Once again, I feared something terrible, and once again there was no need. I was told two people were waiting to see me in the visitors hut. I had received no advance notice. My mother had written to me about Lady Carson's promise to ask her friends in Montreal but I did not know whether she had heard back from them.

Gerald Birks was a dignified, kind gentleman in his early seventies, his handsome wife much younger and smartly dressed.

From the casual way he dismissed the guard, it was evident that he was a retired high-ranking military man. I found out later that at the end of World War I he had the rank of lieutenant colonel.

"Well," Phyllis Birks asked, "how are they treating you?"

"Not bad," I smiled.

"How about the camp school?" the colonel asked.

"It's great." It turned out that as head of the YMCA in Montreal he knew a great deal about it from his friend, the prominent educator Dr. H.M. Tory, with whom he had worked during the war organizing the Khaki University. Dr. Tory, the former president of the University of Alberta and of the National Research Council, had been to Sherbrooke. He had helped to provide resources and establish a relationship with McGill University in Montreal. As a result, our graduating students could be taken to Montreal in heavily guarded buses and take their matriculation exams, which would give them access to Canadian universities.

"Well now," the colonel said, "I think we should get you out in the student category. How old are you?"

"Twenty-two," I sighed.

"I think we can fix that. I understand you're prepared to enlist?"

I swallowed hard.

"Yes, sir."

"Once you're out as a student," he continued, "I think I can get you into a decent regiment."

Just before they left they said they hoped I would stay with them in Montreal until I started university.

On Sunday afternoon, November 9th, I was called out again. This time it was an immigration officer who wanted to ask me a few questions. He was a nice man. He did not mention the age limit of twenty-one. But he raised another obstacle.

"I understand you already have a degree." Cambridge had awarded me a Bachelor of Arts, even though I was unable to sit for the final exam. "Why would you want to get another?"

"It's the only way I can think of to get out of here," I confessed. "Anyway, wouldn't it increase my chances to get a good civilian job to help the war effort?"

"It might."

"I understand the Law School at the University of Toronto has an interesting postgraduate program."

"So," he nodded, "you've looked into that already."

I was far from the first internee to be released from Sherbrooke and had already attended a number of farewell parties for others who had found sponsors, usually through helpful organizations. One, Kurt Swinton, an electrical engineer, had got out as early as February. His mother was in Vancouver and he was sponsored by a former premier of Ontario. Kurt enlisted right away. By October he was a second lieutenant in the Royal Canadian Signal Corps and made a splash visiting his old friends in our sister camp Farnham, in uniform, compelling the sergeant major to salute him.

At the party given in my honour I promised to do all I could to find sponsors for my friends.

On the morning of November 10th, the morning after the interview with the immigration officer, I exchanged my POW uniform for the clothes I had worn in Cambridge eighteen months earlier. A guard took me by truck to the Sherbrooke station with two others whom I hardly knew. It was the first time we left the camp since our traumatic arrival.

We were free.

I had imagined the train trip and the arrival in Montreal for weeks but now that it was happening I had to remind myself again and again that I was not hallucinating.

Colonel and Mrs. Birks were at Windsor Station to pick me up. The driver took my suitcase. Their mansion was on top of the mountain, on Summit Drive, in Westmount. It had a marvellous view — Montreal was at our feet. The driver was also the valet. He had special instructions to make me comfortable in my suite on the second floor.

In due course, Colonel and Mrs. Birks received me in their living room. It was dominated by the statue of a Buddha. The colonel poured me a scotch. Not in my boldest dreams had I tasted a scotch as good as this.

"We have two adopted sons, Otto," Mrs. Birks said. "They call us Captain and Mate. You must do the same."

I looked puzzled.

"You see," the colonel explained. "That's what we are called on our yacht, Captain and Mate."

"Oh," I laughed. "I'll try. I'm not sure it'll come naturally to me."

"I'm sure it will after a while," Mrs. Birks smiled. "My learned sister will study you."

She explained that her sister, Aileen Ross, was a professor of sociology at McGill and had written her dissertation on English Society in Montreal. She was trained to observe people closely.

"Now look here," the colonel said. "Otto is a terrible name. There's a war on. You can't call yourself Otto in Canada, in wartime. Don't you have another name?"

I explained that when I was born I was named Erich. When I was three months old my father died. His name was Otto. So I was named Otto after him.

The colonel was delighted.

"So you're saying you were called Erich at birth?"

"That's right."

"I imagine it's spelled the German way. We'll drop the 'h' and launch you as Eric Koch. That's all there is to it."

"Goodbye Otto," Mrs. Birks beamed. "Hello Eric."